"Jesus said, 'Unless you are converted and become as little children, you will by no means enter the kingdom of heaven.' In a gentle but searching way, R. C. Sproul Jr. helps us understand what Jesus was saying and what it should mean to us today. *The Call to Wonder* is a delightful, yet thought-provoking work. I highly commend it."

JERRY BRIDGES
author of *The Pursuit of Holiness*

THE CALL TO WONDER

Loving God like a Child

R. C. Sproul Jr.

Tyndale House Publishers, Inc.
Carol Stream, Illinois

Visit Tyndale online at www.tyndale.com.

The Call to Wonder: Loving God like a Child

Designed by Jacqueline L. Nuñez

Edited by Susan Taylor

Published in association with the literary agency of Wolgemuth & Associates, Inc.

Library of Congress Cataloging-in-Publication Data

Sproul, R. C. (Robert Craig), 1965-
The call to wonder : loving God like a child / R.C. Sproul, Jr.
p. cm.
ISBN 978-1-4143-5994-6 (sc)
1. Christian life. 2. Faith. I. Title.
BV4501.3.S6655 2012
248.4—dc23 2011047601

Printed in the United States of America

18 17 16 15 14 13 12
7 6 5 4 3 2 1

To Shannon Sproul,

Princess Happy.

Daddy loves you.

And Jesus loves you

Contents

Acknowledgments

IN MANY WAYS this book is born out of childbearing. That is, I want to give to others the lessons I have learned from my eight children. Thanks, then, must begin with my dear wife. While my children show me wonder, my wife *is* a wonder. Thanks are due in turn to each of my children, each of them a joy in our lives.

Not all of my teachers, however, have been children. Thanks are due as well to two of my college professors, Dr. Andrew Hoffecker and Dr. James Dixon. These two men patiently taught this once coldhearted Presbyterian rationalist that the heart of the Christian faith is a changed heart, that sound thinking must move from our minds to our hearts and then out our fingers.

Older still were the teachers to whom my teachers introduced me. Gilbert Keith Chesterton and Clive Staples Lewis continue to inform and inspire me. Each, in their own way, responded to the mechanistic worldview of modernism/naturalism not with cold, abstract arguments but with living words grounded in the living Word. When cynicism comes knocking on my door, I know that reading either of these two great men will send it on its way.

Thanks are due as well to my colleagues for helping to carry a difficult load, and to my students at Reformation Bible College for their zeal.

I am deeply grateful to Robert and Erik Wolgemuth for their invaluable service in coaching, encouraging, and facilitating this project. It is a great blessing to have people in your corner. In the same manner, I want to thank Susan Taylor and Jon Farrar at Tyndale House. Their good work and easygoing demeanor made this project a joy.

Finally, the soundtrack for this book was provided by Palestrina and Pachelbel, the Wintons and Sara Watkins, and Andrew Peterson and Nathan Clark George.

R. C. Sproul Jr.
Thanksgiving Day 2011

Introduction

THIS JUST WASN'T supposed to happen. I tend to be more a thinker than a feeler. And so on that morning, I was taken completely by surprise to find myself crying uncontrollably. Had you asked me that morning, no doubt I could have given you a careful lecture on competing views of just what happens when we come to the Lord's Table. Yet on this day, none of that mattered.

I hadn't been invited to explain anything. I was instead invited to come and participate. We all were. The pastor had reminded us of what Jesus told His disciples on the night in which He was betrayed. And then, row by row, we came forward to kneel and to receive the bread and the wine. My newlywed wife and I walked forward and knelt. The pastor moved along the row, just like normal. This time, however, it was obvious to me that he did not come alone.

Let me explain. I did not have a peculiarly potent sense of my own sin. I didn't see in my mind's eye with special clarity the nails piercing the hands of Jesus. And yet, I began to cry uncontrollably. My body began to shake. It wasn't that this was the first time that Jesus had come to visit us at His own feast, Communion. It was, however, the first time His Spirit had removed the scales from my eyes. Jesus was there with me. It had to be Him. How else could I have, all at once, a razor-sharp dread mitigated by the very lightness of joy? How else could I taste such a crescendo of joy multiplied by the heaviness of dread?

When it was time for us to return to our seats, my wife, puzzled and more than a little afraid, pulled me up and led me back. The service came to an end, and once we began our drive home, she cautiously asked what had happened. I barely heard her. The experience had ended, but rather than leaving me satisfied, it left me hungry for more of God's tangible presence in my life. I wanted to go back to those moments.

I came to learn in the coming years that I couldn't summon these experiences. The Spirit of God is not at my beck and call but rather blows where He will. But I did have that experience again, and then again a few months later. There was no timetable, no way to tell if or when those occurrences of clarity would ever happen again. I could only treasure each one as a signpost that God was powerfully with me, loving and guiding me.

As the years progressed, our family grew, and eventually I planted a church. Now I found myself on the other side of the Communion railing. That was not all that had changed, however. Our little church met in a run-down building. We had no choir, no organ, no heavenly descants being sung. But what I discovered is that God does not reveal Himself only in the trappings of a church service.

It was another ordinary Sunday. I was up front serving the congregation in taking Communion. Having reminded them of Jesus' words on the night He was betrayed, I began to serve my own family. I leaned toward my beloved wife and whispered to her, "The body of Christ, broken for you," and broke down right there. I fell to my knees, the tears began to run, and I hugged her neck, feeling the very arms of Jesus around us both. I managed to move on to my firstborn, Darby. And again there we were, with Jesus right beside us. She felt my desperate hug but was not afraid. She, too, knew that Jesus was there. I turned to my firstborn son, Campbell, who was already crying. As I hugged him, I reminded him that Jesus would never leave him, no matter what battles He might lead us into. Next was Shannon, wondering what all the fuss was about. Her confusion over my response wasn't because she couldn't sense Jesus' presence, but because she feels His presence more fully than I ever will, and does so every day.

Delaney, my inscrutable child, was next in line. From birth she has carried in her eyes a calm that was only beginning to blossom into a gentle and quiet spirit. As I held her and managed to get my voice under control enough to tell her in a fierce whisper, "Jesus loves you, sweetheart, and so does Daddy," she replied serenely, "I know, Daddy."

Next was Erin Claire, the comedienne in the family, whose laughter highlights a haunting sadness in her eyes.

She had, of course, been witnessing this strange event. She knew it was a solemn occasion, and tears began to well in her eyes. "Jesus is here, darling. Right here with us," I told her.

Next was Maili, tiny little Maili. I had to be careful not to squeeze her into nothing. I felt her arms around my neck, and she, too, began to cry. Not from fear, not from sadness, but like Jesus outside the tomb of Lazarus, from empathy. Reilly, barely four, was next. I lifted him over the Communion railing as he wrapped his legs around me. "My son, my son," I said, looking into his eyes. "Do not be afraid, but remember that your daddy loves you, your mommy loves you, and Jesus loves you now and forever." Baby Donovan I picked up also. He dozed through the whole thing, sleeping like a baby. But Jesus blessed him as well.

I had not expected that I would on that day once more be blessed to experience in such an unmistakable way the presence of Christ at His Table. What I swiftly came to understand, however, was not that I needed to find a way to explain to my children what was happening to Daddy so they wouldn't be afraid. Instead I learned that I was to learn from them, that they understood better than I did that He was, indeed, with us. When Jesus said, "Assuredly, I say to you, unless you are converted and become as little children, you will by no means enter the kingdom of heaven" (Matthew 18:3), He wasn't suggesting that our standards are too high and that these little ones can make it over the hump. He was instead telling us that our standards are too low, and that the little ones are far ahead of us.

If you're anything like me, this is one of the hardest lessons to learn. I'm much quicker to assume that my study of Scripture in my office will draw me closer to God and His Kingdom than will spending time in the backyard playing with my kids. Jesus clearly said that may not be the case. And I can't help thinking that one of my most profound experiences of His presence was with my children as we knelt before Him in worship. None of this means that I don't spend serious time studying Scripture and theology. But it does mean that now I take time to stop and watch my kids, noting the things they do that align with Scripture. This book is the result of those times when I paid attention. I sense that as I've contemplated what Jesus meant in His statement above, I have grown better attuned to God's presence in my ordinary, errand-filled days.

My prayer is that this book will encourage you to stop and pay attention as well. My hope is you'll recover the childlike virtues you may have lost and that you'll respond to His call to *become like little children.*

R. C. Sproul Jr.

1

SURPRISED BY GOD

> [Jesus said,] "Assuredly, I say to you, unless you are converted and become as little children, you will by no means enter the kingdom of heaven."
>
> MATTHEW 18:3

DO YOU LIKE SURPRISES? If so, then consider this: God is full of them. And often these God-initiated surprises come in small packages: in the actions and words of children.

The story of the life and ministry of Jesus contains a steady stream of these surprises, twists in the tale, and corrections to our adult thinking that has drifted in the wrong direction.

When Jesus entered the world, who was the first to express joy over His arrival?

It wasn't the religious leaders or the prophets Simeon or Anna.

It wasn't the shepherds or the wise men.

No, the very first expression of joy was from a baby so

young that he had not even been born. John the Baptist leaped in his mother's womb as Jesus, likewise *in utero*, drew near.

A baby in utero. A child.

What a surprise! The great embodiment of the Kingdom of God coming to this earth in human form is appreciated first by a child.

From that point forward, the great Kingdom of the Son of God, Emmanuel—God with us—was expressed within the context of humility rather than in the context of earthly royal glory most of us would expect for God's Son.

Jesus was born in a stable in the backwater of Palestine. Think about it: Jesus—God's only Son—did not draw His first breath in a royal palace surrounded by the splendor that matched His stature. No, His first breath was likely filled with the odors of sheep and cows.

Too many of us adults don't fully grasp the shocking nature of what God's Word says about the living God. We read right over Bible passages that really should stop us in our tracks. Frankly, that temptation is greatest for those of us who have read Scripture many times. We are the ones—the grown-up ones—who tend to tame the God of surprises by explaining away what Scripture clearly says about this living God.

I remember when I succumbed to this temptation. I was at school, preparing for the ministry. My Old Testament professor took the opportunity to teach me a profound lesson that took a while to sink in. I don't remember what prompted his question, but I remember the question clearly. He asked, "R. C., does God have a strong right arm?"

I must confess that I was badly insulted. I wasn't a recent convert. I had read the Scriptures and knew that God is Spirit and doesn't have a body. "Of course not," I replied.

Patiently my professor said, "R. C., the Bible says that God has a strong right arm." I was still a touch insulted, but things were looking up. I thought I understood what the professor was trying to do. He was asking me this simple question so I could give a brief lecture on anthropomorphic language to the rest of the class. I was glad to know that he knew he could count on me to deliver the goods. Perhaps he needed a few minutes' reprieve from teaching and so had handed the ball to one of his most capable students.

"Well, yes, Professor, the Bible does refer to God's strong right arm. But we understand that the Bible frequently uses anthropomorphic language. That is, people sometimes describe God in terms of human qualities that don't rightly belong to Him to help us understand what He really is. The Bible, after all, also says that God's eyes roam to and fro across the earth. What God is telling us is that He is omniscient, that He knows all things. It would be the grossest kind of mistake to think that God's eyes are sitting atop some giant pair of legs and running across the globe like a hamster on a wheel. When the Bible tells us that God has a strong right arm, what it is really saying, speaking as it first did to primitive people, is that God has the quality of omnipotence. He has all power."

I assumed that would settle the matter. Surely the professor would thank me for explaining the concept of God's limitless power so well. Instead, he simply said again, "R. C., the Bible says that God has a strong right arm." The bell rang, signaling the end of that day's class, and I wandered off confused as to what his point could possibly have been.

Years later, God graciously helped me understand what that professor had been trying to impress on me. It is true enough that God is omnipotent. He has all power. There is no power of which He is not the ultimate source. Nothing could ever overpower Him. *Omnipotent*, though, is not the distilled essence of "strong right arm." We do not take the earthy, primitive language of the words *strong right arm* and get closer to the truth by translating it "omnipotent." We actually end up further from the truth. If we were honest, *omnipotent* could simply be a setting on a potency meter, the top line on the ring-the-bell game at the carnival. It tells us how much power God has. If power were illustrated by a pie chart, God would fill it all. What is missing in *omnipotent*, however, that is expressed clearly in *strong right arm* is the idea of purpose and direction. A force could conceivably be omnipotent. It takes a person—no, it takes a *Father*—to have a strong right arm. *Strong right arm* suggests not just how much strength is there but also how that strength functions: it protects, provides, and comforts. Rather than make the strength abstract, as I was foolishly doing in class years before, the phrase *strong right arm* expresses the fact that God the Father is a person. In my so-called sophistication I was not clarifying the message of God but rather diminishing it. I wasn't showing myself to be wiser than my spiritual ancestors. I was showing myself to be a fool.

God is not a nice and reasonable God, one we can tame at will. He doesn't fit into our preconceived notions. As I have learned, we need to stop trying to domesticate the God we are supposed to be worshiping. Instead, we need to understand better the full implications of God's actions and words in Scripture. God does what we don't expect. That's His nature. As C. S. Lewis told us, He is, after all, "not a tame lion."

Here's an example of what I mean when I say we're tempted to domesticate God. Suppose you were an angel watching the tragedy in Eden unfold. You had witnessed the spectacular glory of the creation of the universe. You leaned forward to witness the shaping of Adam and God breathing into him the breath of life. You cried at the beauty of Adam and Eve walking hand in hand in the Garden, only to be even more deeply moved when God joined them in the cool of the evening. Then you watched, your heart in your throat, as the serpent spoke to the woman. You mourned as the juice of the forbidden fruit ran down Eve's chin and then Adam's. You covered your eyes lest you should see the savage destruction when God descended again into the Garden to punish those who had dared to disobey His simple command to not eat of one tree. And then you heard this: "I will put enmity between you and the woman and between your seed and her Seed; He shall bruise your head, and you shall bruise His heel" (Genesis 3:15).

There was no thundering.

There was no volcanic eruption.

There was, instead, a promise, compassion, and hope.

As surprised as you might have been, I suspect confusion would have trumped your surprise. What could God possibly mean that the Seed of the woman would have His heel bruised? As you pondered how God could possibly bring good from this great tragedy, would it ever have occurred to you that the Son of God might become human, take on flesh, and be born of a virgin? Would you ever have come up with the notion that He would take His people's sins on His shoulders? Would you have thought it would be accomplished through the horrors of the Crucifixion? Would you have suspected the wrath of God the Father for sinners like Adam and Eve might be poured out on His Son?

God surprises us. Why? Because, as Isaiah says, God's ways aren't even close to ours:

> "My thoughts are not your thoughts,
> Nor are your ways My ways," says the LORD.
> "For as the heavens are higher than the earth,
> So are My ways higher than your ways,
> And My thoughts than your thoughts."
>
> ISAIAH 55:8-9

The Bible's premiere illustration of how different God's thoughts are from the thoughts of average people is the interaction between Jesus and His disciples in Matthew 18.

Knowing that He would soon face the agony of the Crucifixion and that His disciples' mettle would be tested in the coming days, Jesus began to prepare them for what was coming. First, He revealed His glory on the Mount of Transfiguration. Then He again warned His followers of what was coming: He would be betrayed, and He would die; but He would also rise again.

After all these amazing revelations, the disciples ask, "Who is greatest in the Kingdom of Heaven?" (Matthew 18:1, NLT).

Think about it: Jesus is talking about His coming suffering and humiliation. He is already in an intense battle with the religious power brokers of His day. He is feeling the weight of the cross He must soon bear, already tasting the bitterness of the cup He must drink, and the disciples are asking Him about their chances of promotion when the Kingdom comes! That takes some nerve.

And what does Jesus do? He answers their question. But in doing so, Jesus takes the opportunity to turn the disciples' world right side up. Remember, Jesus isn't talking to His enemies. He isn't talking to the crowds. He is talking to His *followers*. And even His own followers see the world and the coming Kingdom from the wrong perspective.

So Jesus calls a little child to Himself and sets that child in the middle of the disciples and says, "Assuredly, I say to you, unless you are converted and become as little children, you will by no means enter the kingdom of heaven" (Matthew 18:2-3).

We might be tempted to paraphrase Jesus this way: "You want to know who will be greatest? Well, let's see here. First, it won't be any of the grand and glorious among the Roman nobility. Nor will it be the rich and powerful among the scribes and Pharisees." Perhaps at this point the disciples' hearts begin to beat a little more quickly. They are still in the running. "The envelope, please. Yes, the winner of the title Greatest in the Kingdom goes to this little child."

Such a paraphrase would be shocking enough. It certainly would have been strikingly humbling. But that's not what Jesus said. He didn't say that the biggest mansions in the Kingdom will belong to those like children. He didn't say that the ones who are most like children will get to sit at the head table at the marriage feast of the Lamb. The message was far more radical. "If you aren't like this child, you're not even invited. You won't make it past the door. Forget about medals, laurels, and gold-covered thrones. Unless you acquire the perspective, the mind-set, the heart of a child, you will be in the outer darkness: not crying like a baby but weeping and gnashing your teeth."

"The envelope, please. Yes, the winner of the title Greatest in the Kingdom goes to this little child."

Too many of us—I have been guilty of this as well—try to analyze what Jesus is saying and dissect it the way scientists do a specimen they are studying. We take the words of Jesus and run them through our study tools. We check what this scholar thought and what that learned man had to say. We look up key words and how the Greeks used them. We check our cross-references and our systematic theology texts, all in a vain attempt to make the text stop meaning what it is actually saying. Because if it means what it says, it suggests that our knowledge of what this scholar thought and what that learned man said and our ability to wield various Bible study power tools are not just useless but might very easily get in the way. If it means what it says, we would be better off being children. If it means what it says, we are in danger of missing out. If it means what it says, we are going to have to give up either the Kingdom of God or our pride. And both of those things mean so much to us.

All of us do this, of course, because we are sinners, just like the disciples were. This is why I have been working hard over the years to introduce people to what I call "The R. C. Sproul Jr. Principle of Hermeneutics"—in other words, my principle for interpreting the Bible. As you know, there are sound and important rules for how we do this. For instance, we are called to interpret the Bible literally, that is, in terms of its various literary structures. We do not read historical narratives the same way we read poetry. We do not read parables the same way we read historical narratives. All that's pretty basic. The R. C. Sproul Jr. Principle of Hermeneutics is pretty simple: when you are reading your Bible and come across people (like the disciples, for example) doing something really stupid, do not say to yourself, "How could they be so stupid?" Instead, ask yourself, *How am I stupid just like them?* (Note: This principle is named after me because I've learned how stupid I can be.) There is really nothing new under the sun. All of us should expect that the kinds of sins that plagued people in the Bible likely plague us as well. And none is more common than the problem of pride, which often produces stupidity.

Wisdom, the Bible tells us, begins as we fear God (see Proverbs 9:10). Fearing God begins when we believe what He says. When He speaks, we shouldn't seek to wiggle out from under His Word. We shouldn't analyze away the clarity of what He has said. And so it is in Matthew 18. God in Christ tells us that if we are not like children, we will not even see the Kingdom of God. That simply means we had better learn to be like children. We'd better not study how this text can't mean what it actually says. Instead, we'd better study how we can submit to what it means. In the pages to come we will seek to do just that, to consider what childlike faith looks like; to see how, by the power of God's Spirit, we can cultivate the spirit of a child.

The R. C. Sproul Jr. Principle of Hermeneutics is pretty simple: when you are reading your Bible and come across people (like the disciples, for example) doing something really stupid, do not say to yourself, "How could they be so stupid?" Instead, ask yourself, How am I stupid just like them?

Take a long, hard look at the young children in your life—maybe your son or your daughter, maybe your grandson or your granddaughter, a nephew or a niece. Or maybe they're the children who run past you at the mall or in the halls at church.

What does it look like to have a heart that imitates theirs?

What is Jesus asking of us?

Let's find out.

THE MARKS OF INNOCENCE

The LORD is my strength and shield.
  I trust him with all my heart.
He helps me, and my heart is filled with joy.
  I burst out in songs of thanksgiving.
PSALM 28:7, NLT

WHAT DOES IT MEAN to be childlike in our faith? What are the childlike qualities that Jesus calls us to have? And how do we learn to recognize those qualities in children?

When we think of children, the first word that comes to mind is *innocence*. This book describes the kind of innocence Jesus is asking us to imitate. But before I dig into that subject, let me give you a picture of what that innocence looks like and, in the process, give you a preview of where I'm headed.

Most parents, I suspect, have experienced one of those transcendent moments when they see clearly the childlike innocence Jesus is pointing out to His disciples. It happened for me on a bright, sunny day when I glanced out our kitchen window. At the time, my wife and I had six children, the oldest nine and the youngest an infant. As you might expect, we had a great deal of work cut out for us. And although the older children helped out immensely, we still had quite a challenge. There were days when I was simply exhausted.

On this particular day, I had put in a half day's work in my basement office at our country home in southwestern Virginia before heading upstairs to the kitchen for lunch. Because we homeschool our children, everyone was somewhere close by. I peeked out the kitchen window into the backyard and caught a glimpse into heaven. There, roughly twenty feet from the house, were two of my daughters. Delaney, five, who had recently learned to read, was lying down under the shade tree. Leaning up against her, her head on Delaney's stomach, was Erin Claire, age three. Delaney was reading a story to her little sister, who was taking it in with great joy.

The scene was sublime. I was able to take in the peace and joy of two of my little girls. Their security in their surroundings was evident. Though we are living in a world where lions do not yet lie down with lambs, and where children must be warned about the dangers inherent in strangers, for that moment, my two young daughters were caught up into heaven. Though in a sense they were too innocent to be blinded by the glory of what they were in the midst of, I had to turn my gaze aside. It was too much, too beautiful, for my cynical, jaded, fallen eyes to take in.

As I watched my children, for a moment I understood

something of the pleasure our heavenly Father takes in us. How familiar our Father must be with the hardships we all go through. How deeply He must drink of our own pain. He is a God of compassion, of empathy. His zeal to enter into our own hardship was so great that He sent His only begotten Son to take on flesh, to dwell among us, to be tempted in every way we are. On the other hand, He also enters more deeply into the joy we feel than we are able to. We take all these moments for granted, as my children were doing right then, but God Himself enters more deeply into them. He is our Father and ultimately is the source of our joy.

God had made the tree under which my daughters rested. He had created sisterhood, the act of reading, and the stories. And He had brought them all together in this moment of transcendent glory reflected in such an ordinary scene. His love for my daughters dwarfs my own. His delight in their delight was much greater than my joy at the kitchen window when I was overwhelmed by what I saw. The very reason that we can even become like children is because God is so grown up, because He is our Father and we can trust Him.

Have you ever been transfixed by a moment like the one I've described? Have you taken the time to watch how children show their joy for the world God has given them? If you're anything like me, you probably can remember a transcendent moment from your own childhood. What is the moment you remember? Were you staring into the bright blue spring sky? Were you collecting autumn leaves under a backyard oak tree? Were you flying down a hill on your bike? Think back to your own childhood and a time when this life hadn't yet robbed you of wide-eyed enjoyment of simple things.

That's the innocence of childhood. And that's what Jesus is calling us back to.

The first mark we see in children is sheer joy. Children tend to have a rather sunny outlook on life. It doesn't take much to make them squeal with delight: a butterfly, a waterfall, a well-made peanut butter sandwich. Remember that this childlike joy is one of the things that delight our Father so much. Joy is not only what is best for us, not only something commanded by Scripture (see Philippians 4:4), but what brings joy and delight to our heavenly Father. Parents know this. Aren't our happiest moments the ones when our children experience unalloyed joy? That's why we pull out the cameras when our children begin opening presents. We want to capture the memory of such joy for years to come. The memory need not be a moment of stunning triumph, hitting the game-winning home run or taking first prize in the spelling bee. It may be as simple as the joy on a child's face when we offer a word of praise or the delight children express when they are playing with siblings or friends. Our Father in heaven delights in our joy in the same way.

What robs us adults of such joy? It's something children possess in abundance and we adults tend to lack: *sincere trust*. What made that moment at my kitchen window so transcendent was the complete and sincere trust my children showed. They weren't worried about the economy or my next paycheck or friends or housing. They weren't even concerned about where their next meal would come from. Without even thinking about it, they trusted that all those good things would come to them in due time. They were simply enjoying that moment—the gifts God had given them at that time: the expansive oak tree. The companionship of sisters. The joy of hearing a story.

A childlike trust expresses itself most clearly by not thinking of evil. This is precisely what we mean when we speak of the innocence of children. Though they are most assuredly infected and affected by sin, as a general rule, children are ready to believe the best about others. Despite the evident sins even of their own parents, children tend to believe that their parents mean them well, that they are looking out for their children's best interests. Why is this? Because despite the reality of their own sin, children are not driven by crass motives, and they have a terribly difficult time understanding and accepting the crass motives of others. To put it another way, it is difficult to steal candy from a baby not because our consciences trouble us but because the baby is far more likely to give us what we crave without our having to steal it in the first place. Children, in short, enter this world with spirits that are virtually impervious to the mean spirits of others. And that quality is precisely what we are called to cultivate.

This "thinking no evil" attitude that defines what a childlike perspective on the world looks like is rather close kin to the characteristic of trust. In the next chapter, we will see more in depth what trust looks like. But for now, a childlike faith is one that expects others to likewise have a childlike faith. It is secure in its place. It trusts others to mean well. It thinks no evil. That is, it does not look to others with suspicion but instead possesses a deep trust.

Another aspect of a child's innocence is *wonder*, something that is easy for us adults to miss. Too often we are cynical and jaded, in part because we feel as if we have already seen it all. We live in the most media-saturated culture the world has ever known. Hollywood, not content to show us the world as it is, constructs elaborate stories for our entertainment, complete with villains from outer space. Through the years, our eyes and our hearts develop calluses. Only a culture as cynical as ours could have coined that most snarky response to something purportedly shocking: "Been there. Done that. Got the T-shirt."

Because cameras are everywhere and computer animation is able to create ever more outlandish worlds, we say with Solomon, "There is nothing new under the sun" (Ecclesiastes 1:9). Seemingly, everything we could see, everything that could surprise, is already behind us. Unfortunately, this cynical attitude also infects our reading of Scripture. We no longer express wonder at the God who has brought the universe into existence or split seas in two. We've heard those things before—and they no longer inspire our awe.

That's not the case with children. They are built for wonder. They are fresh. Their eyes are new. They have not only *not* seen everything; they have seen virtually nothing at all. Better still, they know how little they are. We look at the stars God made and calls by name (see Psalm 147:4) and see balls of burning gases. Our children, uninfected with such modern arrogance, see them for what they are—God's grand fireworks display—and their eyes are filled with appreciation and wonder. We adults look at a butterfly and ponder the biology of its transformation from a caterpillar and consider the mechanics of its flight. Children see the beauty of a butterfly's colors and feel the gravity-defying lightness of its gossamer wings. Children are quick to gasp, swift to ooh, and eager to aah. They see the world for what it is—a dance, not a machine. Later, we'll explore more of how we can recapture the childlike wonder we've lost.

The last childlike virtue I want to mention is an *eagerness to please*. As a rule, children have neither hidden nor open agendas. They have no specific plans. They are content for the adults in their lives to plan their days. All they ask for is an opportunity to please. Their joy is to bring joy to their moms, to their dads, virtually to any adult within range. How many times have your children asked for your attention as they showed you a new trick or skill they have learned? How many times have they tried to inspire an "ooh" or "aah" from you?

Children are built to please. And Scripture encourages that trait by commanding children to obey. Ephesians 6 begins, "Children, obey your parents in the Lord, for this is right." The command is as clear as it is simple, and our calling to express this childlike quality is likewise clear and simple. Children are not called to clarify their values. They are not called to pursue self-actualization. They are not called to untie various ethical Gordian knots. All children have to do is what they are told.

What does this call to please look like for adults? Let me answer this with a story from my relationship with my own father. Until recently, my family—all our children except the youngest—had spent the vast majority of their short lives in the beautiful mountains of southwest Virginia. That is where our friends live. My children grew up in a church known throughout the country for its close-knit community. Their upbringing, like my own in western Pennsylvania, had been idyllic. But some time ago we packed up our things and left behind our ten acres to go to Orlando, Florida. Our children, especially the older ones, have had a hard time, perhaps because they have missed an important aspect of why we moved to Florida: I moved our family away from all they had ever known because my father asked me to come. He needed some help with his ministry work in Orlando.

Now please don't misunderstand: I did not come to Orlando because I believe I have an obligation to obey my earthly father. Instead, I came here because when my heavenly Father says, "Honor your father and mother that it may go well for you in the land I will show you," I obey my Father in heaven. I moved not in *obedience* to my earthly father but to *honor* him. He asked for my help; I was able to give it, and so, here we are in Florida.

What I saw back in Virginia was the kind of life I wanted to live, surrounded by people I love like family. But my duty was to obey my heavenly Father. He says, "This is how you will live a blessed life." And I have sought to say, "Yes, sir." There is no need to complicate things with questions. God's wisdom doesn't have to make sense to me. I don't need to understand how He will bless me (and my children) through this move. All I need to know is what God tells me to do. And although we would sometimes like to understand those things ourselves, children don't need to be told the hows and the whys.

They can rest contented in the what. I'll explore this concept more later in the book.

For now, suffice it to say that Jesus calls us to unlearn what we've learned as adults.

We've lost our innocence. Our wonder. Our trust. Our desire to please. And we need to regain those childlike qualities.

Daily I witness my spiritual betters in my own children. When the snows came in Virginia, I saw ice crystals falling, slick roads, and rising heating bills. My children sat at the window watching the snow fall, in awe of God's creativity. When nighttime falls and the stars shine, I muse about burning balls of hydrogen. They join the dancing of the spheres in celebration of the God who made them. When our family sits down to eat, I envision a cluttered kitchen and dishes needing to be washed. They see daily bread delivered by their faithful heavenly Father.

Jesus calls us to unlearn what we've learned as adults.

We live in a time when there is no greater social faux pas than the impertinence of being earnest. But our children laugh at no one's expense, dance as if no one were watching, and move through their days buoyed by trust and joy.

We live in a time when there is no greater social faux pas than the impertinence of being earnest. But children laugh at no one's expense, dance as if no one is watching, and move through their days buoyed by trust and joy.

Why would anyone not want to become like a child?

Why wouldn't we want to learn again how to squeal with delight at simple pleasures? to rest completely in God and trust Him with our futures?

I think that was precisely Jesus' point.

The Kingdom of God is filled with these childlike virtues, if only we will learn how to live that way.

3

THE CALL TO TRUST

Lord, I believe; help my unbelief!

MARK 9:24

I REMEMBER THE FIRST TIME I had great difficulty sleeping, a little over seventeen years ago. My problem then wasn't general worries, far less worries about sleeping. The problem was that my house was too noisy. I didn't live above a dance hall or close to the local airport. My challenge was that my firstborn, my little girl Darby, cried all night when we first brought her home. It wasn't that my sensitive ears exaggerated her gentle whimpers. No, my daughter cried long and hard. I held her. I changed her. I fed her. I burped her. I walked her around the living room, trying anything I could think of to calm her down.

Finally, around four in the morning I remembered a tip I had read. I wrapped her up, strapped her in her infant car seat and, although some might frown at this, set the car seat on the clothes dryer and turned it on. Darby went right to sleep. I collapsed on the closest couch and slept too. An hour later both of us were jolted awake by the buzzer on the dryer letting us know our "clothes" were done. But I'm happy to report that it wasn't long before Darby slept well, first in her car seat on the dryer, then in her car seat in her crib, and finally just in her crib. By six weeks she was sleeping through the night. So was I.

It seemed not too long before God blessed us with another child, our son Campbell, and the whole process started over again. Six more followed him, the youngest of whom is now a toddler. This means, of course, that over the last seventeen years I have experienced the challenges of getting babies to sleep in a rather personal way. Existentially speaking, I am therefore puzzled by those who rise bright eyed and bushy tailed to exclaim that they "slept like a baby." Like a baby? Do they mean they woke regularly, fussed and cried, had to be held or fed or burped, and then, after taking a ride on the dryer, were able to get back to sleep? Why do we call a night's peaceful rest "sleeping like a baby"? A "night's peaceful rest" would be the last words I would use to describe a baby's sleeping habits.

It comes down to what we mean by "sleeping." If we mean the hours when other people are sleeping, babies often "sleep" rather poorly. If, however, we mean the actual process or event of sleeping, well that's something completely different. I suspect we describe peaceful sleep as "sleeping like a baby" precisely because when babies are actually sleeping, they look so peaceful. They even look beatific. They are the very picture of peace, contentedness, and satisfaction.

Children usually, or rather eventually, come to trust that their simple desires will be provided for. They trust their moms and dads to meet their needs. While parents may worry about how to keep the wolf at bay, children rarely worry about such things. Consider how the children of the Great Depression typically speak of their experience. They didn't suffer from anxiety. They usually affirm that they weren't even aware that they were poor. When babies are sleeping soundly, they are at peace, confident of their safety and their provision. That kind of childlike trust is what we are all called to.

I remember vividly being shamed by my firstborn along these lines, years after her experience sleeping on the dryer. Our family found ourselves facing some hardships, in terms of both health and finances. I was worried that the children were worried, and I wanted to put their minds at ease. I wanted them to understand that there were assets out there that we could count on, assets belonging to those who loved us and who would not allow us to suffer too severely from the prospective hardships coming our way. So I sat them down and told them about those hardships. I assured them, however, that we would end up okay, even if it meant a relatively spare Christmas. "Do you know why we don't need to worry?" I asked, thinking of those assets. Darby, who was all of eleven, gave the right answer: "Because God loves us."

My goal with this book is for us all to learn to be more like my Darby, to trust our heavenly Father as she did then and still does. What we are seeking is an attitude called *fides implicita*, an implicit faith or basic underlying confidence in the trustworthiness of God. This is, at the very least, how we should trust our heavenly Father.

Consider David. The Bible, of course, doesn't give us a clear affirmation of David's age at the time Israel found itself facing the menace of the Philistines. We do know that David was not yet full grown, that he was still a youth. What delights me about the story is the simplicity of his faith. You remember the story. The army of Israel is camped on one hill, the army of the Philistines on the other. David's three oldest brothers are serving in the army, while David remains home caring for the flocks. There is not much fighting going on. Instead there is the constant boasting and challenge of the champion of the Philistines, Goliath. The text describes vividly his fearsome size and weaponry:

> A champion went out from the camp of the Philistines, named Goliath, from Gath, whose height was six cubits and a span. He had a bronze helmet on his head, and he was armed with a coat of mail, and the weight of the coat was five thousand shekels of bronze. And he had bronze armor on his legs and

> a bronze javelin between his shoulders. Now the staff of his spear was like a weaver's beam, and his iron spearhead weighed six hundred shekels; and a shield-bearer went before him.
>
> 1 SAMUEL 17:4-7

For forty days Goliath laid down a verbal gauntlet, shaming the army of Israel, defying them, and insisting that they send down their own champion. When David is sent from home with more food to find his brothers in the army, he does not come with a careful strategy. He doesn't notice a chink in Goliath's armor and devise an elaborate plan to exploit it. His confidence isn't found in superior thinking, far less any sort of physical advantage. His assumption is as clear as it is basic—this man Goliath is challenging not just David, not just the Israelite army, but the true and living God. Though Goliath is bigger than David and every other man in the army of the Israelites, he is not bigger than God. God will give the victory.

When David descends into the valley, having rejected the armor and weaponry of King Saul, Goliath taunts still more.

> When the Philistine looked about and saw David, he disdained him; for he was only a youth, ruddy and good-looking. So the Philistine said to David, "Am I a dog, that you come to me with sticks?"
>
> And the Philistine cursed David by his gods. And the Philistine said to David, "Come to me, and I will

> give your flesh to the birds of the air and the beasts of the field!"
>
> I SAMUEL 17:42-44

David, however, is not in the least bit worried. One can almost imagine that he is actually encouraged as more taunts come from the enemy. David knows that the God of heaven and earth is hearing every word. Better still, David knows that God is altogether trustworthy, and so he responds:

> You come to me with a sword, with a spear, and with a javelin. But I come to you in the name of the LORD of hosts, the God of the armies of Israel, whom you have defied. This day the LORD will deliver you into my hand, and I will strike you and take your head from you. And this day I will give the carcasses of the camp of the Philistines to the birds of the air and the wild beasts of the earth, that all the earth may know that there is a God in Israel. Then all this assembly shall know that the LORD does not save with sword and spear; for the battle is the LORD's, and He will give you into our hands.
>
> I SAMUEL 17:45-47

David didn't go out to do battle. He went out to witness what God would do. Like Joshua before him, he knew that the battle belonged to the Lord. David's only calling was to be faithful. The results were in God's strong right arm. The moral of the story is not that David was so heroic. The virtue that drove David was not courage or bravery. He went into that valley because he trusted God as a child trusts his father. He had an implicit trust that God was looking out for him. That, more than the death of Goliath, is the victory.

The patriarch Job, of course, is anything but a young man when we meet him in Scripture. And God does not deliver him as He did David. God instead hands Job over to Satan. Job loses his wealth, his health, and his family. He is not only given over to Satan to be tormented, but his friends, and even his wife, prove to be additional burdens to him in his trouble. Job, unlike David in his youth, is not constant in his trust. But he stands firm for some time, even making this most trusting affirmation: "Though He slay me, yet will I trust Him" (Job 13:15).

Note, however, how God responds when Job can no longer contain himself, when he loses that implicit trust. For two long chapters God answers Job. His answer, however, isn't to tell Job about God's conversation with the devil. He doesn't even give Job a lengthy exposition of how suffering works for our good and teaches us patience. Instead, for the length of those two chapters God speaks of Himself, His power, His wisdom:

> Then the LORD answered Job out of the whirlwind,
> and said:
> "Who is this who darkens counsel
> By words without knowledge?

Now prepare yourself like a man;
    I will question you, and you shall answer Me.
Where were you when I laid the foundations of
        the earth?
    Tell Me, if you have understanding.
Who determined its measurements?
    Surely you know!
    Or who stretched the line upon it?
To what were its foundations fastened?
    Or who laid its cornerstone,
When the morning stars sang together,
    And all the sons of God shouted for joy?
Or who shut in the sea with doors,
    When it burst forth and issued from the womb;
When I made the clouds its garment,
    And thick darkness its swaddling band;
When I fixed My limit for it,
    And set bars and doors;
When I said,
    'This far you may come, but no farther,
    And here your proud waves must stop!'
Have you commanded the morning since your
        days began,
    And caused the dawn to know its place,
That it might take hold of the ends of the earth,
    And the wicked be shaken out of it?
It takes on form like clay under a seal,
    And stands out like a garment.

From the wicked their light is withheld,
    And the upraised arm is broken.
Have you entered the springs of the sea?
    Or have you walked in search of the depths?
Have the gates of death been revealed to you?
    Or have you seen the doors of the shadow of death?
Have you comprehended the breadth of the earth?
    Tell Me, if you know all this."

JOB 38:1-18

God's answer is that He is bigger than Job. He affirms just how little Job is, how childlike he is. The argument isn't that God is a supreme being and Job only a created being and therefore Job has no moral place to stand in his complaint. God isn't pulling rank. Neither is He suggesting that Job's mind is simply too small to understand that God's thoughts are not our thoughts. He is instead affirming, demonstrating through the glory of the creation, His unfathomable trustworthiness.

In other words, we cannot trust God too much. His word is trustworthy not just because He is good, because He is wise, because He is far too moral to ever tell a lie. Rather God cannot tell a lie because the very nature of reality is interwoven with what comes out of His mouth. That is, He cannot lie because His words create reality. I learned this truth in college. A young and popular professor on campus had invited me to participate in a Bible study he was hosting. There were ten young men there each week. The teacher explained that he had handpicked us because he was so confident that we could change our campus. I can't say for certain what his motives were, but that statement certainly played into my own pride. So one evening, when he asked what appeared to be a rather silly question, my pride rose to the challenge. He asked, "R. C., what would happen if God were to say to you, 'R. C., you are a car'?"

I took the opportunity to explain how the universe would implode upon itself because the whole ordering principle of the universe was tied up in God's character. If He could lie, the universe could not hold together. The teacher brushed aside my answer, so I tried another response. "Well, if God said I was a car, then we would know that the Bible was not true, and so all our hopes would be dashed. It would mean that when God says, 'Believe on the Lord Jesus Christ and you will be saved,' that, too, might be a lie."

"No," my professor explained, "that's not what I'm looking for. R. C., if God said, 'You are a car,' your hands and feet would turn into tires. Your chest would instantly transform into a piston engine. Your eyeballs would morph into headlights." We can trust God implicitly because His word is to reality what Midas's touch was to gold. He speaks, and it happens.

Jesus drove this point home when He was teaching His disciples to pray. The disciples wanted Jesus to teach them to pray, just as John the Baptist had taught his disciples to pray. So Jesus told His disciples, "When you pray, say: Our Father in heaven" (Luke 11:2). I often wonder if the disciples even heard the rest of the prayer. If I had been there, I suspect my mind would have blown all its fuses with that first phrase. Jesus is telling us to speak to the Maker of heaven and earth, to address Him as our Father. We are His children. We do not pray, "Oh Grand Exalted One . . ." Instead we speak to our Father who loves us as a father.

John makes much the same point when he says, "Behold what manner of love the Father has bestowed on us, that we should be called children of God!" (1 John 3:1). Lest we dismiss this as semantics, lest we think that the work of Christ merely makes us honorary members of the family of God—that is, merely *called* the children of God—John goes on, "Beloved, now we *are* children of God" (v. 2, emphasis added). That is what we are. Our Father is the self-existent One, the Creator, who made all things. That's our dad. How could we do anything other than trust?

Even our sins do not mar or destroy His love for us. Any wrath our Father might have toward our constant sin was dealt with almost two thousand years ago. I know that of all the earthly fears I have ever had, one stands above all the rest. Despite my earthly father's constant love and encouragement, I always have feared that I would somehow disappoint him. My heavenly Father, however, is never disappointed in me. Because of Christ, I am His son, in whom He is well pleased.

As He did with Job, my heavenly Father allows pain in my life, but He always does so for my own good. This is another reason why He is the great Physician. Doctors may sometimes hurt us, though whatever pain they may cause is for our good. Once, a doctor had to ask me to be the bearer of pain. Our fourth child was roughly two and a half or three years old when, unbeknownst to us, her curiosity created a challenge. While playing on our living room floor, she found a tiny little bright blue circle, no more than a centimeter in diameter. It was a part to a bigger toy. My little girl was apparently so curious about what this little disk might smell like that she stuck it right up her nose.

Eventually her nose began to bother her, so we took a look. And there we saw that little circle each time she exhaled. When she inhaled, it went back up into her nasal cavity. We tried everything we could think of to get it out, but nothing worked. So we trudged off to the doctor's office. Our family doctor also was unable to retrieve the pesky blue squishy thing. Our next stop was the emergency room. The ER doctor tried this thing and that, pulling out ever increasingly frightening-looking tools. Finally, he came up with a brilliant idea—reverse mouth-to-mouth. That's where I came in.

The doctor instructed me to close off the unobstructed nostril. I whispered to my little girl not to be afraid, that Daddy was trying to help her. Though there was fear in her eyes, she lay still. The doctor told her to open her mouth, instructed me to put my mouth over hers, and told me to blow. My breath—and the obstructive object—came out her left nostril. My little girl had to trust me, just as I had to trust the doctor. And she was made well. She didn't need a complicated explanation of what was going on. She didn't seek "informed consent." It was enough that her dad asked her to do it, because she knew that she could trust him.

Children find this kind of trust quite natural. We are under the care of a Father who not only loves us but is also all-powerful. This means not merely that all His power is sufficient to defeat every other power but that every other power is dependent upon Him for its very existence. All power is ultimately His. And He has promised us that "all things work together for good to those who love God, to those who are the called according to His purpose" (Romans 8:28). When we are caught up in our troubles, when we are overwhelmed with sorrows, we tend to think that this text is clichéd, that it is inappropriate for our context. But the hard truth is that nothing could be more appropriate.

He knows all that is happening in our lives. He knows it, however, not because He watches it happen. God is not all-knowing merely because He sits on high witnessing everything. God is all-knowing first because He is no mere spectator. He wrote history before any of it even happened. Better still, God is like Shakespeare. He wrote the story, but He also wrote in parts for Himself. That is, God acts in space and time. This is why David faced Goliath with such confidence. God was walking with him, just as God had planned it. That is why Job could trust Him, because the events of Job's life were all planned from before time and because God walked with Job.

When hardship comes, therefore, we know that God has chosen it, even gift wrapped it for us, for His greatest of purposes: that we would be made more like His Son. His goal, thankfully, isn't that we would be comfortable. It isn't that we would enjoy a life of ease. Rather He is determined to do the most glorious thing for us that He could possibly do. He is remaking us into the image of His Son, who is the express image of His glory. He is teaching us to trust Him, even as His Son trusted Him, even unto death. Though God the Father slayed Jesus the Son, yet Jesus trusted Him.

When I was a small boy, it was not unusual for my father and mother to invite seminary students to our house for dinner. The dining room was bursting with theological table talk. My father is a veritable font of wisdom, and these students had come to listen. Sometimes, however, perhaps to squelch any doubts they might have about him, or more likely for comic relief from the heavy conversation, my father would ask me a theological question: "Son, who wrote the Bible?" I answered with the utmost certainty—and to the laughter and delight of the rest of the table, "You did, Daddy." Though not every child has a theologian for a father, children do tend to think their fathers know everything. When their daddies tell them things, no matter how improbable, aren't they quick to believe?

Consider the idea of Santa Claus. Some parents tell their children that there is a man living at the North Pole whose only passion is making toys all year long. This man is able to tell which children have been naughty and which ones have been nice. He is supported in his labors by a vast army of elves. And once a year, empowered by a team of flying reindeer, this man manages to make his way into every home on the planet, delivering toys to all the children and, of course, taking the time to sample the cookies we leave out for him. But it isn't the magic of the story that makes it so attractive to children. It is the power of a parent who makes the unbelievable believable.

Children, by and large, are lacking in doubt, in skepticism, in unbelief. They believe what we tell them. My firstborn son was born in Florida. He was raised in southwest Virginia. He has no immediate ties to western Pennsylvania. Yet his heart is committed to the Pittsburgh Pirates baseball club, the Pittsburgh Penguins hockey team, and especially the six-time Super Bowl Champion Pittsburgh Steelers. Why? There are, of course, careful, rational, well-thought-out arguments in favor of the objective superiority of the Pittsburgh Steelers. But that is not why my son believes in them. It is because this is what I have taught him, loyalties that my father taught me.

The apostle Paul connects this kind of childlike trust to the calling all Christians have to love one another. In the famous "love chapter," 1 Corinthians 13, among the attributes of love is this one: "[Love] thinks no evil" (v. 5). Grown-ups are quick to think the worst of others in large part because of how well we know ourselves. We suspect others of ill motives, of evil thinking, because that is precisely what we are guilty of. Children, on the other hand, have more guileless spirits. They think no evil. They trust others because they assume that those people mean as well as they do.

That said, even as he closes his exposition on love, Paul in turn deals with the call to maturity. We will be looking at this at some length later. Let me be clear: the call to be trusting, to be guileless like children, is not an invitation to allow ourselves to be hurt. I am well aware that the Bible not only calls us to be like children, but it calls us to be "wise as serpents, and harmless as doves" (Matthew 10:16, KJV). There are genuine dangers out there that we and our children need to be aware of. There are, on the other hand, times when our trust is betrayed, when we are hurt precisely because we have trusted. We have to make choices, and although our broader culture pushes us in the direction of doubt, God calls us to deeper trust.

Consider this story about Thomas Aquinas, the great scholastic theologian. The story takes place well before his reputation grew to where it is today, when Thomas was still a student. Not yet known as Dr. Angelicus, as history would remember him, Aquinas had another nickname. His classmates called him the Dumb Ox. This gentle giant was gifted with a titanic intellect, but he was still considered slow. His classmates found it amusing to mock him, including his extraordinary ability to trust.

The story is told of a prank Thomas's classmates played on him. For some reason, he was late getting to the classroom. The professor was not yet there, and the rest of the students all gathered around the classroom's window, craning their necks, trying to get a look outside. When Aquinas entered the room, he naturally asked what all the fuss was about. His classmates explained that there was a herd of pigs flying through the sky right outside the window. As Thomas hurried toward the window to get a better view, his classmates fell aside and burst into uproarious laughter. The harder Thomas looked, the harder his classmates laughed.

Finally Thomas understood that he had been the victim of a prank. As his classmates got their laughter under control, one asked him, "Thomas, did you really believe that pigs could fly?" Thomas had the last laugh when he answered humbly, "I find it easier to believe that pigs can fly than I do that my classmates would lie to me." If we refuse to have the faith of children, we will never fall victim to such lies. If we adopt a skeptical "show-me" perspective on the truth claims of others, we will certainly filter out any number of whoppers. But we will also miss out on experiencing childlike innocence. And we will make the world a darker, more sinister place.

If we refuse to have the faith of children and adopt a skeptical "show-me" perspective on the truth claims of others, we will certainly filter out any number of whoppers. But we will also miss out on experiencing childlike innocence. And we will make the world a darker, more sinister place.

My goal here is not to reduce your skepticism about me. I am not your father. I am not my father. And I am most certainly not the Father. We ought, in fact, to be most on our guard with those who are the most zealous about getting us to trust them. The world is full of great men and women who will disappoint us. All our heroes have feet of clay. I know my children have reason to be disappointed in me. I know more than I would like about some of my own theological heroes. We are an altogether untrustworthy bunch.

The call to trust like children is the call to trust our Father in heaven. This trust is not something we have done only once, when we first came to saving faith—something we signified at church camp by throwing our pine cone into the fire, or when we walked the aisle, or said the sinner's prayer. This trust is not something that brings us peace with God and then we forget about it. It is the same trust we are called to as we grow in grace and wisdom. We are to trust God in our sanctification the same way we do in our justification. Of course we are called to cooperate with the Spirit as we become more righteous. But we cooperate with the Spirit best as we more deeply trust in the Father, as we cry out like the father of the son who was deaf and dumb, "Lord, I believe; help my unbelief!" (Mark 9:24).

We cooperate with the Spirit best as we more deeply trust in the Father, as we cry out like the father of the son who was deaf and dumb, "Lord, I believe; help my unbelief!" (Mark 9:24).

We trust best, I believe, when we take the time to study, to remember God's trustworthiness. I face a peculiar challenge when I open my Bible. As a professor, it is all too easy for me to see the Bible simply as a book to be studied. To be sure, I believe it is a unique book, God's inerrant, infallible Word. But I can still see it as an object of study rather than as a book that studies me. When the Bible is the object of my study, I forget whose child I am. Because

I have been brought into the family of God by the power of the Holy Spirit and the life and death of the Son, God's book is now my family history. By faith I am a child of Abraham, which means that when God delivered Abraham, when He proved Himself faithful in leading Abraham from Ur of the Chaldees, He showed Himself faithful to my family.

When my father Abraham walked with my brother Isaac toward Mount Moriah, he did so as God's child, trusting his Father. As Abraham raised his knife to kill his son, the son of the promise, even though no one on the planet had ever been resurrected, even though everyone who died thus far had stayed dead, even though God Himself had said nothing about resurrection, Abraham believed. He trusted. That is my family's story.

My brothers and my cousins walked out of Egypt after four hundred years of slavery, still under heavy burdens. But as they left, they were carrying the gold, the silver, and the precious jewels of Egypt that were now theirs. And when the army of Pharaoh came after them, and their backs were to the Red Sea, those who had faith like children did not cry out that they were doomed, that God had forsaken them. Instead they were filled with giddy anticipation, wondering what miracle God would work next.

My brothers and cousins Shadrach, Meshach, and Abednego trusted God as children trust a faithful father and refused to bow before the statue of Nebuchadnezzar. And they demonstrated their trust in a most peculiar way. They did not tell the king, "Wait until you see what our Father is going to do for us. You're going to want to watch closely." Instead, they affirmed two great and trusting truths: God might save them (He had the power to do so). But He might not. It made precious little difference to the three young men. And our Father sent our elder Brother to walk in the flames with them.

Finally, Stephen was my uncle. His story is my story. When he had faithfully preached the good news of Jesus Christ, he was not rescued like Shadrach, Meshach, and Abednego. No, he was rescued in a completely different way. The stones were thrown, and Stephen lost his earthly life. But before he died, Stephen was given a glimpse of the Judge of heaven and earth standing in his defense. And Stephen trusted.

God has given us these stories not just to study but to *believe*. These are our family stories. And each time, each and every time, God proves to be utterly and completely trustworthy. That is His nature. He is our Father, who loves us and always, *always* does what is best for us. Therefore, He calls us to trust Him, every moment of every day. May He give us the grace to reply with joy, "Yes, Daddy."

4

THE CALL TO WONDER

The heavens declare the glory of God;
and the firmament shows His handiwork.

PSALM 19:1

NEWBORNS ARE FASCINATING to me. I wish I knew how it's possible to understand what is going on inside the minds of those who cannot yet speak. Though I am baffled as to how they could reach their conclusions, I once read that some scientists believe (or at least did believe—these things tend to change quickly over time) that newborns are unable to distinguish themselves from the world around them. In other words, according to this theory, newborns don't know where they end and their blanket begins. They don't know, even when we are holding them, that we are something apart and distinct from them. Their identity encompasses all that their senses are able to take in.

Can you imagine what that must feel like? I know what it's like to have difficulty believing that something is really you. When I look at my waistline, which doesn't stop where it should but insistently marches right past my belt, I have some sense of being bigger than I am. When my head grows right through my hair, I have something of the same sensation. But no matter how much hair I lose, no matter how much weight I might gain, I know there is an end to me.

Happily, of course, even if the theory about newborns is correct, babies eventually come to understand their own limits. What though, must *that* be like? Do they feel themselves shrinking? Do they, at six months of age, look at their blankets with a sense of longing and nostalgia? Do they think to themselves, *I remember when we were so close it was like you were a part of me. What happened between us, Blankie?*

As strange as the incredible shrinking world of the newborn must be, how much stranger is the exploding world of the just-born baby? The womb is certainly a comforting and safe place, but it is also a cramped little world. If babies were able to blog, I suspect they would not have an awful lot to say—"Today I changed positions and pushed against reality's walls. Tomorrow I will likely do much the same thing." But their world changes immensely at birth. Their world expands from the womb to, well, the whole world. They have seen only hints of light, have heard only muffled sounds. But now the whole world opens up before them. Suddenly they are not too big for the world but far, far too small.

Consider how our lives might be shaken if someone

discovered not aliens but humans living on the dark side of the moon. Imagine that we found there not a people more sophisticated than we, that might have built flying ships eons before the rest of us. No, these are a primitive people. Remember that it took far longer for Columbus and his men to sail across the ocean than it took astronauts to travel from the earth to the moon. It wasn't, in the case of Columbus, just a new land mass that was found, but a land mass populated by human beings, bearers of God's image.

Would such a discovery make us all at least a little more skeptical about what we think we know? Wouldn't we all lose at least some confidence in those things we are now most sure of? If the world could be that much different from how we perceived it, shouldn't we be slower to trust our own perceptions of reality?

Finding out we're not alone and finding out we're not as smart as we thought we were could take us in one of two directions. We could certainly pout. We could become cynical, treating the created order as if it had cheated us by hiding part of itself from us for so long. We could refuse to affirm, to believe, anything. We could consider ourselves too in the know, too sophisticated, too grown up to believe in anything.

The other option, however, would be to delight not only in what we learn about the world, but to delight in what it tells us about ourselves. We could rejoice in the fact that we aren't quite as smart as we thought we were, that the world is not only much bigger than us, not only much bigger than we thought, but that it has more than a few tricks up its sleeve. We could see the world for what it is—a glorious manifestation of the glory of our Maker. If we serve a God of surprises—and we do—and if His creation is a reflection of what He is, then we should not be surprised to find that His creation is full of surprises. And that should elicit in us a sense of wonder.

C. S. Lewis once again provides great wisdom here. In his essay "Meditation on a Tool Shed," published in a collection of essays, *God in the Dock*, Lewis explains a moment of insight he had in his own tool shed. He describes how the sunlight shone through a gap in the door, providing a sliver of light in which could be seen elements of the shed, but through which also the outside world could be seen. The ray, or band of light, he explains, is not the end of our seeing, though it can be seen. Rather it is the source of our seeing. By the light we are able to see.

The same is true with respect to the creation. It is not the end in itself. It is, however, that by which we see, not just the creation, but the Creator. Consider David's words about what the creation says to us:

> The heavens declare the glory of God;
>   And the firmament shows His handiwork.
> Day unto day utters speech,
>   And night unto night reveals knowledge.
> There is no speech nor language
>   Where their voice is not heard.
> Their line has gone out through all the earth,
>   And their words to the end of the world.

In them He has set a tabernacle for the sun,
Which is like a bridegroom coming out of his chamber,
And rejoices like a strong man to run its race.
Its rising is from one end of heaven,
And its circuit to the other end;
And there is nothing hidden from its heat.

PSALM 19:1-6

We show our own cynicism—our lack of childlike wonder—when we run our eyes over these words and reduce them to an argument about what theologians call *natural revelation*. Some like the notion that God reveals Himself through nature. Others are against it. And so these words of Psalm 19 become a kind of theological football, a text to support one side and a text to be overcome by the other side. We think the text is telling us something as modernist as this—that the astonishing design elements of the created order speak to the reality of the Creator. The world is a rather sophisticated clock; that means there must be a clockmaker.

Now the creation clearly and unambiguously speaks of the necessity of a designer. But do we really think this is what David was trying to tell us? Was David writing a psalm or poem to be used as a tool in a battle against Darwinism that was thousands of years in his future? Or were David and the Holy Spirit seeking to communicate something that is at the same time even more basic and more astonishing?

That the heavens declare and the firmament speaks is not coincidental to what they are. I speak—I speak a lot. But even if I were to become mute, I would still be me. My speaking doesn't define me. But the universe speaks because that is precisely what it was made for.

Most of us at one time or another have looked into the night sky and wondered why God would make such a mammoth universe just for us. The answer to that question is simple: He didn't. Oh, He made the universe, but not for us. He made it for Himself, to make His glory evident.

When David celebrates the fact that the days utter speech and nights reveal knowledge, what knowledge is being revealed? The psalm gives the answer at the beginning. All the stars in all the galaxies, all the electrons orbiting every nucleus, say the same thing—*God is glorious; God is glorious.* The more we are like children, the more we will have ears to hear that refrain and hearts filled with the wonder of it all.

All the stars in all the galaxies, all the electrons orbiting every nucleus, say the same thing—God is glorious; God is glorious. *The more we are like children, the more we will have ears to hear that refrain and hearts filled with the wonder of it all.*

Ironically, one of the ways we miss experiencing wonder at the glory of the Creation is found in how we seek to describe that glory. We rightly ascribe glory to God for how He has designed the universe. We are rightly impressed with how things fit together, how the universe "works." Have you ever heard someone explain how planet Earth is tipped on its axis in just the right way? That if you were to tilt the earth just one degree more toward the sun, we would be a flaming ball of fire, and if you tipped it just one degree away from the sun, we'd be a frozen ball of ice? It's true, and it is glorious, but it assumes something we ought not to assume—that God in His role of creator is merely behaving like an engineer.

Engineering is a wonderful field. I am terribly grateful for the gift engineers have been given, never more so than when I am being carried to far-off places in a well-engineered flying machine. Engineers, though, operate in a world full of givens. That is, they design things to fit the world as it is. When they build a bridge, they have to take into account heat transfer rates of concrete and the tensile strength of the iron rods they use. They even have to take into account the impact of harmonics, as movement created by vibration could adversely affect the strength of the bridge. I can't begin to fathom all the considerations within which they work.

God, however, had to take nothing into account. The astounding thing about the creation of the universe isn't how wonderfully God put the parts together. There were no parts. There were no rules. God could have made a sun that threw off coolness rather than heat, that made everything dark rather than light. He could have made a world just like ours, except backward and inside out. God didn't "have to" tilt the world this way. He didn't "have to" tilt it that way.

The universe is not some kind of clockwork, something that looks as if it has life and vitality but on the inside is just a machine. It is no machine at all. No, the universe is a dance. It operates the way it operates not because of a need for efficiency but because of God's desire to show forth beauty. God is not an engineer and the universe a machine. Instead God is a choreographer and the universe a dance. God's universe shows us who God is, and so a response of wonder toward the universe leads us to a deeper sense of wonder about Him.

Wonder, in short, is a profound experience of how small I am and how big God is. This is different from a deep knowledge of the difference between us and God. The distinction is subtle, but it is important. Were we to quiz evangelicals across the board and ask them this simple question, "Is God profoundly bigger than you are?" I suspect everyone would get the right answer. There is no subculture in the church, no parachurch ministry with this as its defining commitment: "I'm pretty big, and God isn't so big." We all know in our minds that God is big. The Westminster Shorter Catechism asks this question: "What is God?" It answers this way: "God is a Spirit, infinite, eternal and unchangeable in His being, wisdom, power, holiness, justice, goodness and truth." Infinite is plenty big. And God is unchangeably infinite in His being. We all also know in our minds that we are small.

The trouble is that there is often a disconnect between our heads and our hearts. Our lips say we are small, but our hearts think we are great. Consider Eve. Here she was, walking about in a paradise that was made in the space of six days. She knew that she was a new creature, that she had more in common with the ants in the Garden than she had with the One who made her, the ants, and the Garden. Her brain was unclouded by sin. But still the serpent was able to seduce her with this outlandish promise: "You shall be as God" (Genesis 3:5). Eve was hungering to grow up, and to do so before her time. A child would have laughed at the notion.

Wonder, then, isn't merely the knowledge that God is great and we are small. It is instead *the joyous embracing of this truth*. It is curiosity about this great gap, seeing it not as something to resent but something to celebrate, to play in. Consider snow. That's right, snow. The adult sees snow one way and the child a completely different way. An adult homeowner may see work and danger and expense. Commuters tend to trudge through the snow hunched over, trying to bury their heads in their chests. Children see it completely differently. Have you seen their eyes as they look out the window watching snow fall? Children walk through the snow with their faces toward the sky, their tongues hanging out, hoping to catch a flake. Adults sigh when they see snow. Children gasp for joy.

Wonder isn't merely the knowledge that God is great and we are small. It is instead the joyous embracing of this truth.

Snow is the ultimate marriage of complexity in harmony. Billions upon billions of unique notes fall together in a crescendo of white unity. If you should ever be blessed to be far enough from the cacophony of civilization when a heavy snow falls, you can even hear the very music of the iced dew's delicate descent. It is the repainting of a landscape in a thousand hues of white. It is the dance of the wind. It is as if, just for a time, we get to enter the wonder of Narnia, or of

Middle-earth, to dance amidst the miracle of liquid manna. Indeed, when the snow begins to fall, I imagine God as a sort of celestial Tom Bombadil, from The Lord of the Rings, walking and whistling through His heaven, reaching deep into His pockets for fistfuls of joy to drop on His creation.

In snow we see the extravagance of creation, remembering again that God made the universe for His glory. Creation, after all, must have been a plenty cool thing. The angels, I'm sure, took their seats with a level of anticipation we can only imagine as they waited for the curtain to go up. God said, "'Let there be light'; and there was light" (Genesis 1:3). That must have been something. The radiance broke forth, and the heavenly chorus sang. Glory!

As I struggle with the remnants of modernism in my own thinking, I, too, tend to see the glory of creation in the design stage. I find it easy, as we have noted, to think of the universe as a staggering marvel of engineering. I think that after the angels saw the light, God took a time-out to explain the wave properties and the particle properties, and how He balanced them in an almost incarnational way. (Jesus is, after all, the Light of the World.) Like a scientist explaining an experiment, like a detective explaining a crime, God dispassionately explained His secret blueprints. I think that this is God's pleasure in the creation, that He is tickled pink with His own elegance.

This is all well and good. The universe is quite the harmonious complexity of a watch, and our Lord quite the skilled Watchmaker. However, I believe that when I do a better job of thinking like a child, the universe, in the end, is not so much an astounding machine as it is a way-yonder too-much-fun toy. It is God's toy, and His delight in it is like that of a child. The trees in the fields clap their hands, not as solemn applause but as giddy frolic. The seas roar, not like a lion but like the crowd at the football game. The mountains melt not because of a consuming fire but from the very looseness of joy. And then there is snow, an extravagant array of tiny ice sculptures coming together to form a falling curtain on the earth. No machine could ever do that. A toy, on the other hand, a planet-sized snow globe, that's something God could not only make but also play with for months on end. A hurricane allows us a tiny peek at the terror of the Lord. But falling snow invites us to be still and know that He is God or, better still, to laugh with Him in giddiness over His creation.

As a modern man, I, too, am tempted to think that by taking a thing and breaking it down into its constituent parts, I will grow closer to understanding what it is. But if you take a rose and carefully take it apart, if you slice its petals razor thin and put them on a slide under a microscope, you are getting further from understanding the rose, not closer to it. The "roseness" of the rose is not found in its DNA but in its beauty. The same is true of the whole of the universe. Of course there is a place for scientific study. But it is not the only place.

Jane Austen got at what I'm trying to say in one telling conversation in her classic work *Pride and Prejudice*. A ball is being planned, and Caroline objects:

> "I should like balls infinitely better," she replied, "if they were carried on in a different manner; but there is something insufferably tedious in the usual process of such a meeting. It would surely be much more rational if conversation instead of dancing made the order of the day."
>
> [Her brother responds,] "Much more rational, my dear Caroline, I dare say, but it would not be near so much like a ball."

When we think of stars merely as burning balls of gas in the sky, we are making a terrible categorical mistake. I am more than willing to concede that stars are made up of various elements. But that is not what they *are*. In fact, the Bible says that God "counts the number of the stars; He calls them all by name" (Psalm 147:4). The stars sang in response to the glory of the creation: "When the morning stars sang together, and all the sons of God shouted for joy" (Job 38:7). How foolish I am that I would be tempted to pat God on the head for coming up with a pretty metaphor, to think myself so much more sophisticated than the psalmist or Job, to think that my *scientific* understanding of the universe is closer to the truth, closer to God's perspective on His own creation.

When God puts on a show, it is not His intention that we sit with furrowed brow, pencils in hand, and seek to discern what creates the colors in the Northern Lights and how large the solar flare was that caused them, or that we can map the trajectory of lightning flashes, or measure the decibels of the thunder's crash. What we're supposed to do is squeal with delight. We're supposed to clap and giggle. We're supposed to gasp in wonder and ask for more. We're supposed to respond with expectancy at the magic of it all, "Oh, do it again! Do it again!" We're supposed to take in the universe the way a child naturally takes in a fireworks show. That we fail to do that is not a sign that we've grown up but that we have grown cold and lost a childlike wonder.

Now, it would be enough that God should be so big and we so small. The display of His glory in the universe is enough to make us stay young until we are old. There is magic enough to keep us giggling and asking for more. The greatest wonder, however, is that the one who performs all these incredible feats is our Father who knows us and who loves us. The great and spectacular display of His glory isn't something that we just happened upon, as if we were walking home after a hard day at school and heard the sounds of a circus parade down Main Street. What we discover is this: all the magic, all the power, all the glory rests in the hands of our Father, the one who has adopted us into His family.

David describes this spirit of wonder and awe in one of his more familiar psalms. I'm afraid, however, that our familiarity with the psalm reflects our familiarity with the creation. It seems to our tired ears that David is allowing his emotions to get away from him. The truth of the matter is that David is straining because the words just aren't big enough for the reality. See what he says:

O Lord, You have searched me and known me.
You know my sitting down and my rising up;
    You understand my thought afar off.
You comprehend my path and my lying down,
    And are acquainted with all my ways.
For there is not a word on my tongue,
    But behold, O Lord, You know it altogether.
You have hedged me behind and before,
    And laid Your hand upon me.
Such knowledge is too wonderful for me;
    It is high, I cannot attain it.

Where can I go from Your Spirit?
    Or where can I flee from Your presence?
If I ascend into heaven, You are there;
    If I make my bed in hell, behold, You are there.
If I take the wings of the morning,
    And dwell in the uttermost parts of the sea,
Even there Your hand shall lead me,
    And Your right hand shall hold me.
If I say, "Surely the darkness shall fall on me,"
    Even the night shall be light about me;
Indeed, the darkness shall not hide from You,
    But the night shines as the day;
    The darkness and the light are both alike to You.

For You formed my inward parts;
    You covered me in my mother's womb.

I will praise You, for I am fearfully and wonderfully made;
Marvelous are Your works,
And that my soul knows very well.
My frame was not hidden from You,
When I was made in secret,
And skillfully wrought in the lowest parts of the earth.
Your eyes saw my substance, being yet unformed.
And in Your book they all were written,
The days fashioned for me,
When as yet there were none of them.

How precious also are Your thoughts to me, O God!
How great is the sum of them!
If I should count them, they would be more in number than the sand;
When I awake, I am still with You.

PSALM 139:1-18

How ironic that David connects the heights of the glory of God with the making of the human body. Truth be told, there is no greater manifestation of the glory of God in all the created order than you and me. God invites us to see the world as children in part by giving us children. When my dear wife, Denise, and I celebrated our nineteenth wedding anniversary in 2011, we spent time reflecting upon the nearly two decades of our life together. Over those nineteen years we certainly had our challenges. Between us we have had four separate bouts with cancer, including the battle we are currently going through. We have had work setbacks and the sudden loss of dear friends. But what is most astonishing to me is that nineteen years ago when we said, "I do" there were just the two of us. Now God in His grace and glory has added to our number. We were two, and we are now ten, and we will now forever be.

I sit at my dining table and fight back tears because I get to live the blessing of Psalm 128:

> Blessed is every one who fears the LORD,
>   Who walks in His ways.
>
> When you eat the labor of your hands,
>   You shall be happy, and it shall be well with you.
> Your wife shall be like a fruitful vine
>   In the very heart of your house,
>   Your children like olive plants
>   All around your table.
> Behold, thus shall the man be blessed
>   Who fears the LORD.
>
> The LORD bless you out of Zion,
>   And may you see the good of Jerusalem
>   All the days of your life.
> Yes, may you see your children's children.
>
>   Peace be upon Israel!

These children were not, but now they are. And I am falling into the modernist's erroneous thinking if I say they came here merely through natural processes. If I reduce the whole process to the birds and the bees, I miss the beauty and glory of God orchestrating our conception of six of those eight children as well as His orchestrating our two adoptions. Of course, ultimately He controls all things—from the rise and fall of nations to the descent of a single leaf in autumn. But here, He bends over backward to remind us that He forms our children and puts homeless children in families.

There are the circles in circles that multiply the glory of the dance. I get to sit at a table and watch my firstborn delight in her younger brother. I get to see him drink in the joy of the five-year-old. I get to see my thirteen-year-old establish a bond with her littlest brother, and he with her. I get to see my two youngest girls delight in each other and also welcome their new brother into their world. I get to experience this reality—not the exasperating, wallet-stretching, energy-draining view that I have eight—*eight*—children. No, I get to live in a world with my beloved wife, with Darby, Campbell, Shannon, Delaney, Erin Claire, Maili, Reilly, and Donovan. I may be the dad, but I am a kid in a candy story, a candy store owned and stocked by my heavenly Father who loves me.

I *get to* . . .

What do you *get to* do?

5

THE CALL TO PLEASE

Jesus said to them, "My food is to do the will of Him who sent Me, and to finish His work."

JOHN 4:34

To BEARD OR NOT TO BEARD? That has been the question more than once in my life. Roughly a year after my wife, Denise, and I and our first two children had moved from Orlando to southwest Virginia, we found ourselves blessed with Shannon, our third child. In God's good timing, my parents were planning to visit, and my father would be able to assist me in baptizing my little girl as I served the small church I was planting. In the few weeks between the baby's birth (and the corresponding lack of sleep) and their visit, I grew a beard. I knew my father wasn't a fan of beards, so I planned to shave mine off the day before his arrival.

But in thinking through my desire to honor my father, I came up with an even better idea. Rather than shave before he arrived, I would wait to shave until after he had arrived and would let him know that I was doing this to honor him. When he arrived and I told him that I was going to shave it off for him, he graciously encouraged me to keep it.

So the beard stayed with me for the next nine years until, in the summer of 2006, it literally fell into my keyboard. I was writing an article on my laptop and noticed the steady descent, whisker after whisker. It wasn't much of a surprise to me. I had been going through chemotherapy as treatment for Hodgkin's lymphoma. I hadn't noticed the hair falling off the top of my head as much as my beard disappearing because there hadn't been much hair on my head to begin with. But when it rained whiskers, it poured.

By the following spring there was no sign of lymphoma in my system. The chemo had done its job, and slowly the beard made its way back. This time it lasted for four years. In the interim I had been through some radical changes. My father asked me to move my family away from rural southwest Virginia and the church I had planted there, away from the only home my children had known, away from what I sincerely believe to be the greatest church family on the planet, to come and help him at Ligonier Ministries.

It was not all that difficult a decision. Painful, yes, but not so difficult. My wife and I were confident that moving was the right thing to do. Our reasons were simple: when your father asks for help, the way to honor him is to help. And my Father in heaven tells us that the way to have a good life, the way for things to go well for us in the land, is to honor our fathers and mothers.

The move was hardest on my oldest children. They had invested their lives in the people of our church community. They had owned and embraced the theological commitments of the church. They had deep friendships, not just with their peers but with whole families. As hard as it was for them, though, they all did their best. They put on stiff upper lips. They prayed for strength, patience, and understanding. They sought prayer support from their friends. Everyone stayed calm and peaceful, albeit sad. Sadness turned to anger, however, when my beard came off once more.

My father had expressed his view that it was something of a hindrance to my work and that it would be wise to shave it off. I did not agree with his reasoning at all. But I did agree that it was wise to shave it off because he asked me to. That set off my oldest. She was puzzled. She was hurt. She was angry. She expressed her concern in a way that honored me, but there was little question of her feelings.

I reminded her how difficult and painful it was for me to move the family. I reminded her about how we reached the conclusion that it was something we ought to do. And so I asked her, "If I was willing to move us all away from the life we enjoyed in Virginia in order to honor my parents, then wouldn't I be that much more willing to do something as easy as scraping the whiskers off my face? I borrowed a poker analogy: "When it comes to the fifth commandment, sweetheart, I'm going all in. I'm betting it all on God's promise that this is the way to have a good life. I'm not smart enough to figure out the right path to joy. But I know who is. And He says that those who honor their parents can expect it to go well for them in the land."

One could argue that my perspective is rather crass, a carefully calculated cost-benefit analysis. If I do X, the most likely result is Y. Children, I believe, have a far simpler way of calculating whether or not to do something. They have a much simpler goal. One of the defining qualities of a child is this—that they are eager to please.

There are myriad theories on child rearing both inside and outside the church. Some are infused with more biblical wisdom, some with more worldly wisdom. In the discussions Christians have, however, I remember hearing one objection to one theory that made no sense to me whatsoever. Whatever the theory was that was being propounded, it covered how to train children not to do this or that. The objection was that this or that is natural, and that it is therefore unnatural and wrong to try to train the child out of it. In raising eight children, I have come to know what natural looks like, and it's not so good. When we speak of something being natural, we have to ask, "Which nature?"

When we are going through difficult times, is it natural to grumble some, to complain a little? Yes and no. That is, this temptation seems reasonable to us because of our fallen nature. But we are being remade. Both Paul and James tell us to rejoice when hardships come, not to grumble and complain. Our old nature finds it natural to complain. Our new nature ought to find it unnatural to do so.

Sin isn't something that gets introduced into our lives sometime after we pass through puberty. Sin can encourage even young children to see themselves as the center of the universe. This is "natural" for all of us, but something we are all called to put behind us. Despite the reality of sin, however, there is something innocent about children, or Jesus would not have told us to be more like them. We have to understand this innocence in a way that doesn't deny the sin we all struggle with, whatever our age. And we have to understand the reality of sin, even in children, in such a way that we don't hold on to a wrong notion of innocence.

Despite the reality of sin, there is something innocent about children, or Jesus would not have told us to be more like them.

In chapter 3, we examined children's propensity for trust. This demonstrates a kind of innocence. Because children tend to not be given to grand self-interested schemes, they tend to assume the same about the rest of us. Just as there is confusion in my own mind over what we mean by "sleeping like a baby," I also wonder why we describe something profoundly easy this way: "It's like stealing candy from a baby." It's actually, at least in my own experience, rather a difficult thing to steal candy from a baby. Not because children are so zealous in guarding what is theirs, but precisely because they are not. You can't steal candy from a baby because babies are so eager to give away what they have.

One could argue that this propensity for trust is one place where the image of God is less marred in the young than it is in the old. That we all, young and old, are sinners doesn't mean necessarily that we all face the same kinds of temptations with the same intensities at all times in our lives. Trust is something most children tend to hang on to, even with sin present in them.

In like manner, the posture of wonder, in which we experience deeply the contrast between God's greatness and our smallness, in which we celebrate that "little ones to Him belong," seems natural, in a good way, to children. It is fitting for them to take in His bigness and rejoice in it. That joy finds its completion, however, in the glorious truth that the glorious Creator of the glorious creation is also our Father. Just as a child naturally looks to the strength of his earthly father in trust, just as a child naturally stands in wonder and awe of his father, so we, the children of God look to our heavenly Father.

There is another normal, or natural, response that children have to their experience of the bigness of their fathers—they aim to please. Again, as the father of eight children, I get to experience this reality virtually every day. For most of my time as a father I have enjoyed what is happily becoming more common in the modern workplace—my workplace has been my home. Despite my constant proximity to my family, I nevertheless get the full treatment when I come "home"—when I leave my work space and join the rest of the family. Right now it is my ten-, nine- and five-year-olds who respond as if they thought I would never return. "*Daddyyyy!!!!*" they shout as I come down the stairs, racing to hug me and to be hugged.

But it doesn't end there. After the hugs they are eager to tell me about their day, to show me what they did during their schooltime, to give me the pictures they have drawn for me. It is a beautiful thing. These are not insecure children desperately seeking the approval of others. They don't do this to receive. Instead they do it to give. Their desire to please isn't ultimately for their own pleasure, but for the pleasure of those they please. They delight in delighting their parents because of their natural joy, not because of some kind of fear of rejection.

This ties back to trust. Children have a delightful presupposition that others will automatically like them, not because someone has persuaded them that they are particularly likable, but rather, because their natural response to others is to like them. Adults, at least this adult, sometimes begin new relationships with suspicion and competition. Children begin new relationships with trust and wonder.

This same principle works in reverse. If anything could darken the sunny disposition of a child, it is this—the fear that they might somehow disappoint us. But just as the desire to please is driven by security, not insecurity, by the desire to give, not by selfish motives, the same is true here. That is, a child fears to disappoint a parent not because it would upset the child, but because it upsets the parents. Children are sad when they fail, only because they know that their failures make us sad.

The Bible regularly gives us twin paradigms that end up creating "chicken and egg" problems. Consider the relationship between husbands and wives. The apostle Paul, in the letter to the church at Ephesus, gives an extended comparison about the relationship between a husband and wife and the relationship between Jesus and the church. This raises the question, Did God give us marriage in part to serve as a living, breathing metaphor for the work that Christ would come to do, or did God simply seize upon an already existing reality to help us understand a new reality?

The marriage relationship is not the only earthly one that teaches us about a heavenly relationship. The relationship of parents and children parallels the relationship of our heavenly Father with all those who are His in Christ. Though as with the husband and wife relationship, the analogy is imperfect because of sin, there are still important things to learn from that human relationship.

On the other hand, there is yet another biblical example that sheds even more light on human relationships, as well as on our relationship with our heavenly Father. That is, God is not only a Father to us, where our sin can muddy up the picture, but He is also the Father to the Son. The Bible says that Jesus is "the firstborn among many brethren" (Romans 8:29). It says that we are "joint heirs" with Him (Romans 8:17). If we want to understand how we are called to relate to our heavenly Father, we would be wise to study our elder Brother. For even though Jesus is our elder Brother, He is childlike in exactly the right way—perfectly, sinlessly so.

Of course one of the first things we notice about this relationship is the passion the Son has to please the Father. Skim through the Gospel of John and see if this doesn't jump out at you. What drives Jesus is less a passion for rescuing us and more a passion to do the will of His Father in heaven. When the disciples returned from their mission to secure food and found Jesus in conversation with the Samaritan woman at the well, they offered Him some of the food they had brought:

> At this point His disciples came, and they marveled that He talked with a woman; yet no one said, "What do You seek?" or, "Why are You talking with her?" The woman then left her waterpot, went her way into the city, and said to the men, "Come, see a Man who told me all things that I ever did. Could this be the Christ?" Then they went out of the city and came to Him.
>
> In the meantime His disciples urged Him, saying, "Rabbi, eat."
>
> But He said to them, "I have food to eat of which you do not know."
>
> Therefore the disciples said to one another, "Has anyone brought Him anything to eat?"

> Jesus said to them, "My food is to do the will of Him who sent Me, and to finish His work."
>
> JOHN 4:27-34

Jesus describes how important it is to Him that He does His Father's will—it is His meat and drink. This is how He survives; this is what He lives on. This passion, however, did not end with the ascension of Christ. He is still about His Father's business. To help us understand how that is so, we need to stop a moment to take a bird's-eye view of the whole Bible.

How would one rightly summarize the Bible? Some have suggested that the Bible is a "boy meets girl" story. That is, the whole of the Bible is the account of how Jesus secures His bride. In favor of this perspective is this observation: broadly speaking, the Bible begins and ends with a wedding. In the beginning Adam and Eve are brought together as husband and wife. In the end we see the marriage feast of the Lamb, as Jesus, the second and final Adam, rejoices with His bride, the second and final Eve—the church of Jesus Christ. If anything pictures the glory of heaven, it is this beauty, that there the church will feast with her Husband. This wedding is the mother of all weddings, the reality of which all others are but a shadow.

If this summary is a touch too romantic for you, consider this outline of the Bible:

Genesis 1–2: Creation
Genesis 3: The Fall

Genesis 4—Revelation 22: Trying to get back to Genesis 1 and 2, only better

That last point is important. The history of the world is the history of the Second Adam succeeding where the first Adam failed. Adam and Eve enjoyed sinlessness. They enjoyed the presence of God. They enjoyed peace in the Garden. The Second Adam is bringing us to the place where we will enjoy sinlessness, where we will enjoy the presence of God, where we will enjoy peace. The "only better" part is that now we enjoy these things in and through the death of Christ on our behalf. The Second Adam won the battle when all the odds were stacked against Him. And He did it to please His Father.

Whichever story we take for our summary though, we recognize that both have a beginning and an ending. But with neither of these two summaries have we reached the final end. There is still more to come. The Bible tells us that having died and risen, secured and purified His bride, Jesus has one thing more to do. The real climax of the story is described in 1 Corinthians 15:20-24:

> Now Christ is risen from the dead, and has become the firstfruits of those who have fallen asleep. For since by man came death, by Man also came the resurrection of the dead. For as in Adam all die, even so in Christ all shall be made alive. But each one in his own order: Christ the firstfruits, afterward those

> who are Christ's at His coming. Then comes the end, when He delivers the kingdom to God the Father, when He puts an end to all rule and all authority and power.

The true end of the story comes when the Son delivers the Kingdom to the Father.

Several years ago the ministry I founded hosted a conference. In fact, we put on a conference every year for several years. Each year I found myself dealing with a level of nervousness I wasn't used to. When I speak at someone else's conference, my job is simply to teach or to preach. As a conference host, on the other hand, I am ultimately responsible for what everyone says. I am responsible for seeing that everyone has a place to sit, that everyone can hear what is said, that the speakers have their needs met, and that the event does not end up awash in red ink.

One particular year, however, the weight of responsibility was nearly unbearable. I wasn't merely nervous in the sense that I had butterflies in my stomach. I was nervous enough to not be able to sleep at night. I wasn't worried about logistics or about what the other speakers might have to say. I wasn't even particularly worried about how the audience might respond to what I had to say. What worried me was what one speaker in particular might think about what I had to say.

The title of the conference was *Generations: Giving Honor to Whom Honor Is Due*. We wanted those attending to understand the biblical truth that as we honor our parents, and all those in authority over us, it will go well for us in the land (see Deuteronomy 5:16). One of my guest speakers was my friend Doug Phillips. I knew he would do a wonderful job, knowing him to be not just a man of integrity but also a man filled with respect for his father. His father was another one of our guests. But it was the third guest who worried me, not because of what he might say, but because of what he might hear. That third guest was my father.

Doug and I thought it would be a good idea not just to teach on how to honor our fathers but to demonstrate how we can do so by honoring our respective fathers in front of everyone. As I considered my own nerves, I came to understand that the issue was much broader than just the conference. As I began to look back over the history of the ministry I had started a decade before, I realized that things were more complex than I had understood. The purpose of our ministry was and is to help Christians live more simple, separate, and deliberate lives for the glory of God and for the building of His Kingdom. That expresses our corporate reason for being and defines the message we proclaim. But it profoundly misses the real motive in my own heart. Of course I long to see Christians live such faithful lives. But I gradually began to understand that every article I wrote for our magazine, every lecture I gave at one of our Bible studies, every couples camp we hosted, every pastors camp we held, every Basement Tape we recorded, every conference we held, every chapter of every book I ever wrote, was ultimately a dead mouse on my father's porch.

Let me explain. When I moved to southwest Virginia, I dipped my toes into the life of a gentleman farmer. I purchased mail-order chicks to raise, some for eggs and some for meat. It was not long before their dead carcasses were littering my property. Every raccoon, possum, and fox viewed my little farm as the destination for its own personal buffet. So we got a dog. The dog kept the other critters away, but not because she was faithful about her responsibilities. The truth was that she didn't like the competition. Within a week of Socks's arrival, she broke into the portable pen that housed our growing meat hens and killed all twenty-five of them. She didn't even have the decency to eat her kill. She just left the mess for me to clean up.

I mention all this to explain how I look at animals. They are wonderful things, as long as they contribute and remember their place. We did not keep pets. We kept working animals, and their place was outside. We had a few cats as well, and they, too, lived outside, in part because they couldn't do their job inside—keeping rodents away. They weren't pets; they were mouse hunters.

That said, this doesn't mean that we had no emotional connection with our animals. We loved our chickens—with gravy. We loved our dog, Socks, despite her sins. And despite cats' reputation for being too cool to care, we know all of our cats loved us. We know this because of the mice we would find on our back porch. Working cats are not content to quietly and invisibly do their job; they want you to know they're working. When they capture a mouse, a rat, or a mole and have put said creature to death, they carry the carcass to the back porch, as if to announce, "Look what I have done for you, my master." On some level I saw my own work at Highlands, in part, in the same way. I wanted my work to please my father and honor him.

I understand that I have sometimes failed to please my heavenly Father and will continue to fail from time to time. And I certainly don't want anyone to hold my earthly father accountable for everything I ever said, wrote, or did. On the other hand, our example, the Son of God, never fails. His perfect life and His continuing work delight our Father in heaven, which in turn delights the Son. As He returns a perfected Kingdom to His Father at that last moment in history and we enter into the rest of the story, our elder Brother exhibits just what it means to be a child eager to please His Father.

Some people would point out that I may have won the parent lottery, that having my father be not only my hero but the hero of many others has distorted my perspective. I'm aware that not all of us have had admirable and respectable earthly fathers we are so eager to please. All of us do, however, have a Father we are called to be eager to please. However hard our upbringing might have been, whatever strains there might yet be, even whatever regrets we might have over our relationships with parents who have passed on, we also have a Father who lives forever. And if we are His, we have a Father who loves us forever. The desire to please Him, then, isn't something unique to me. It is, at its root, human, even though distorted and colored by our sin.

This is the reason that when the Bible speaks specifically not just *about* children but *to* them, the first thing it tells us is to obey. This is what defines us—that we are children who are called to obey, called to please our parents. In Ephesians 5 and 6, Paul gives some brief instructions for the health and obedience of the whole family. Wives are called to be subject to their husbands as unto the Lord. Husbands are called to love their wives sacrificially, just as Christ loved the church and gave Himself for her. Then Paul directs his attention to the children, telling them, "Children, obey your parents in the Lord, for this is right" (6:1). That's fairly succinct, isn't it? Why should children do this? Because it's the right thing to do. It is what children were made to do.

However hard our upbringing might have been, whatever strains there might yet be, even whatever regrets we might have over our relationships with parents who have passed on, we also have a Father who lives forever. And if we are His, we have a Father who loves us forever.

Paul continues by giving more reason why this is wise: "'Honor your father and mother,' which is the first commandment with promise: 'that it may be well with you and you may live long on the earth'" (Ephesians 6:2-3).

This is how we lead the good life. This is where obedience leads us. This is the gracious promise of our heavenly Father. Sin begins with the temptation to *not* seek out what pleases our Father. And redemption ends with our pleasing

Him eternally with our worship. This is the child's version of the statement by John Piper, who reminds us, "God is most glorified in us when we are most satisfied in Him." Our heavenly Father delights in nothing more than our joyful delight in seeking to please Him, to do His will. Too often, unlike the generous and giving spirit of children, we come to the law of God wondering, *What is the minimum we have to do in order to stay out of trouble?* We wonder if He is really watching. Or we look at His law as a burden. I am tempted to see my own obedience not as a child would but as a debtor would. That is, I think, *Well, God does say not to do this. And since He did redeem me, since He did save my soul, I suppose I'd better not do what He wants me not to do.*

Children don't typically think in those terms. We ought, instead, to see our attempts at obedience to God's Word the way a child looks at learning to ride a bike. Of course we fall down. Of course we scrape our knees. But for every foot of progress, for every push of the pedal, for every successful, albeit wobbly, turn of the wheel, we rejoice because we know that He who held us, who bandaged our skinned knees, who helped us get back on the bike and gave us another push, is grinning from ear to ear as we learn to ride.

A simple life is really not related to raising chickens. A truly simple life is one that sets aside the lesser goals that distract us from the one main goal. Like children, we do not have to fight some grand battle or solve a great mystery. All we have to do to live a simple life is to live with this simple goal: that all we do, all we think, and all we say would please our Father in heaven. All we need to do is take delight in pleasing Him, and we will find, as Psalm 16 says, "pleasures forevermore."

When Jesus calls us to be childlike, He is, in effect, calling us back to that simple goal and desire we lost when we became adults: the ardent desire to please. He yearns to see us once again run to Him exclaiming, "Look, Daddy! Look! Look what I've done!"

6

THE CALL TO OUR FATHER

Behold what manner of love the Father has bestowed on us, that we should be called children of God!

1 JOHN 3:1

IT WAS CERTAINLY not the only time I had ever put my foot in my mouth, but I suspect it had never before been in so deep. Our dear friends had just added another blessing to their family. When we first met them, they had two teenaged boys and a little girl who did not look like the rest of the family. Mom and Dad had been born in Virginia, and the sons in Maryland, but the daughter had come from Korea, joining the family through the blessing of adoption.

A few years later the family added another daughter, a sweet little baby who had been born in India and had also come to the family via adoption. Still, I managed not to embarrass myself just yet. It was the family's third adoption that proved fatal to me. This time they adopted a little boy born in America. His ethnic ancestors, however, hailed from Africa, so his melanin levels didn't match his parents'. That wasn't how or why I slipped up. Rather, in seeking to communicate our common spirit and affirm my own family's shared zeal for the blessing of adoption, I announced to the proud mom of now five children, "I can't wait until my wife and I are old so we can adopt."

I know. Cringe worthy. I'm grateful to say that she forgave me, though I suspect she hasn't forgotten. Neither did God forget. Though I'm not exactly sure where one draws the line on "old," my dear wife, Denise, and I found ourselves just a few years later ready and eager to adopt. My bride's battle with breast cancer left us, as far as we could tell, unlikely to ever conceive again. God had already blessed us at that time with six children, the oldest of whom was eleven. The reasoning behind my verbal gaffe was simple. Believing children are a gift from the hand of God, Denise and I would welcome as many as He would send. When we suspected that He would send us no more through more natural means, we would see if He might bless us through adoption.

We had plenty of examples all around us. Many families in our church had adopted. Our little congregation at that time numbered about one hundred souls representing fewer than twenty families. We lived and worshiped in Mendota, a tiny town in rural southwestern Virginia, population three hundred. About a third of our families had been blessed with children from countries all over the world. We had not just

Koreans and East Indians but also Russians and Filipinos, Haitians, and Africans. When our little church gathered, we looked like a miniature United Nations. We were almost certainly the most ethnically diverse Christian church for hundreds of miles around, right there in rural Virginia.

Denise and I began the process. We filled out a mountain of papers. We attended classes. We had social workers come and visit our home. We had letters of recommendation sent by family, friends, and pastors. We put together a photo album describing our home life and our community. (In many circumstances expectant moms are permitted to study these albums to help them choose the family with which they would like to place their child.) We had our backgrounds checked by the police. We wrote a fat check, all to get to the point where we would be considered worthy to adopt a child. At that point we had to hope and pray that we would find a baby.

Our local social worker put us in touch with an adoption agency in Arkansas that ministered to moms in crisis pregnancies. We sent out our information, including our photo album, and waited—although not patiently. My wonderful bride was just the kind of woman to plow through the whole process, to make sure all our papers had their i's dotted and their t's crossed. She kept us on schedule and kept the whole process in order. While our "package" was in the mail, however, an event happened that not even my wife could control. Hurricane Katrina hit.

The resulting chaos kept our package from reaching its

destination in Arkansas on time—just as God had planned. Because of that delay, my wife was constantly on the phone with the agency, checking almost daily to see if everything we had sent had arrived. Those constant calls kept us on the agency's radar. Days later a birth mom in labor released her son to the agency, leaving the choosing of adoptive parents up to them. My wife was out running errands, preparing for a family camping trip, when the call came in. When she got home, lugging groceries into the house, I explained to her, "I'm sorry we won't be able to go camping this weekend. Instead we're going to be driving to Arkansas to pick up our son." What an odd blessing, that I as the husband got to announce to my wife, "We're going to have a baby."

We drove, over two days, to Arkansas, where we met our precious little guy, Reilly Justice Sproul. He was less than five pounds and all legs. Under the legal arrangements, we were permitted to care for him while we waited for our day in court. So for roughly a week the three of us stayed and waited for our turn, which would turn out to be the most surreal part of the entire experience.

The courtroom was mostly empty. There was a bailiff, the agency attorney, the head of the agency, the judge, Denise, Reilly, and me. We stood before the judge as he mingled small talk with what I presume were legally required questions. It was all very warm and pleasant. But then he asked his last, and by far oddest, question. He wasn't quite stern, but he was serious as he asked us, "Now you understand, don't you, that when I sign these papers and bang this gavel, this boy will be your son, as much your child as any of your other children? If something were to happen to you two, whatever would happen to your other children would happen to him. He is not to be treated any differently. He will be your son."

I honestly didn't know what to say. As far as my mind could grasp, the judge was asking a question the answer to which was so obvious that he must have meant something else. It was as if he were saying, "Now you understand, don't you, that the sky is blue and grass is green?" Wouldn't you think such a question must be code for something else? Realizing that he was being utterly sincere, and realizing that sarcasm was not the fitting response, I managed to get out, "Yes, sir" and leave out, "That's why we're here." We came to bring a son into our family. We couldn't imagine anything less—Reilly is a blessed addition to our family, and we are thrilled and grateful to have him.

Happily, others have shared our joy and from time to time have put their feet into their own mouths. Given my own history, rather than get angry at such verbal missteps, I like to have fun with them. We are now a family of ten, having also added Donovan Deaun to our family through adoption. Like his older brother Reilly, Donovan has an ethnic background that stretches back to Africa. And so we are often asked about them: "Are they brothers?"

To which I happily reply, "Of course."

Some people question further: "Do they have the same mother?"

To which I happily reply, "They certainly do."

And some go further still: "Do they have the same father?"

"I'm happy to report that they do."

"Were there any other siblings?"

"Well," I reply, "there are actually six other siblings, and they are a part of our family as well."

Others seem to race to the punch line, asking when they see all eight of our children, "Which ones are yours?"

To which we delightedly respond, "All of them."

The glory and the beauty of adoption touch on what happens when we face something we're not used to. We think babies come from the hospital, when sometimes they come from the airport. We think parents have the same skin tone as their children, but sometimes they don't. We think once you pass a certain age, you won't have any more children, when you just might. Families grow in different ways, which doesn't make them any less families.

The Pharisees once made a lame attempt to trip Jesus up. One of their lawyers asked simply what the greatest commandment is. And Jesus answered straightforwardly. Then Jesus turned the tables on His questioners.

> While the Pharisees were gathered together, Jesus asked them, saying, "What do you think about the Christ? Whose Son is He?"
>
> They said to Him, "The Son of David."
>
> He said to them, "How then does David in the Spirit call Him 'Lord,' saying:

> 'The LORD said to my Lord,
> "'Sit at My right hand,
> Till I make Your enemies Your footstool'"?
>
> If David then calls Him 'Lord,' how is He his Son?"
> And no one was able to answer Him a word, nor
> from that day on did anyone dare question Him
> anymore.
> Matthew 22:41-46

The Pharisees have nothing to say. They've been casting about with questions, but now they are caught in one. Their dilemma is clear—Jesus makes it clear—"If David calls Him 'Lord,' how is He his Son?" What is interesting is that Jesus Himself does not give the answer. He doesn't explain how this could be, how one man could be both another man's son and also his lord.

For Christians, of course, there is at least one obvious, albeit implicit, answer. We know that the one of whom David spoke was unique in all of human history. He was not only a man but also the first and only man ever to be God in the flesh. The Incarnation gives a powerful answer to the question. Jesus, in His humanity, is the son, the descendant, of David. In His deity, however, Jesus is not just the Lord of David but His Maker. And not just the Maker of David, but the Maker of all things. We can answer the question by remembering the two natures in the one person of Jesus Christ.

The Bible is abundantly clear that Jesus was both God and man. The creeds that we have been blessed with over the first five hundred years of the church post-Resurrection especially, carefully and faithfully delineate what we can and cannot say about this amazing reality. Consider what we say about Jesus and the Incarnation in the Nicene Creed: we confess with the church through the ages that Jesus is "begotten, not made."

Many of us may tend to glaze over when we hear these words, thinking that such language is a glaring contradiction that does nothing more than give us a charley horse between the ears. How can we make sense of it? *Begotten* we understand. *Made* we understand. How someone could be one and not the other, however, is difficult to understand. But thinking about the nuances and subtleties of adoption may help.

We would not want to affirm that Jesus was a creature who was "adopted" into the Trinity. Instead, we want to remember that words can be understood from different perspectives. We have fallen prey to an erroneous mind-set if the only way we can imagine someone being made a son is by procreation. And we have fallen into the same error if we think the only way one could be "begotten" is to be made.

In both instances we need to walk more deeply into what it means to be called a son. Sonship is so much more than the result of being conceived. It is even more about a relationship. God the Son is not called God the Son because He had a beginning in space and time (being made). Instead it is because He is called to obey as a son, to love and to be loved as a son. This goes back to the idea we talked about in a previous chapter. Though the Son (and of course the Spirit) is equal to the Father in glory, holiness, power, and in every perfection, He nevertheless takes on a submissive role to the Father, delighting to do His will. He takes on the role of the firstborn Son, of the Heir. He is the obedient One.

These images exist not just to tickle our brains but to teach us important truths about what it means to be not just a child but a child *of the Father*. Our calling ultimately isn't merely that we would be like children but that we would be like *His* children, that we would be the sons and daughters of the Maker of heaven and earth.

God has made the brilliant stars. He has made the magnificent mountains. He has spoken galaxies into existence and spun the webs of atoms together. But He has called none of these creations His children. We alone, unlike the animals and the angels, are called His children. If we have been born again, remade, adopted, then we alone have been given the privilege of being called His children.

If we are in Christ, we have been blessed far beyond the forgiveness we have in Him. God has done far more than declare us to be not guilty. He has adopted us into His family: "Behold what manner of love the Father has bestowed on us, that we should be called children of God!" (1 John 3:1).

When I was ten years old, I won a contest. My name was drawn, and I was chosen to serve for the then Super Bowl Champion Pittsburgh Steelers as their "Mascot of the Week." I was invited to practice at the stadium, where I was given a tour of the offices and the locker room. I had pictures taken with six future Hall of Famers. The day of the game my picture was in the program, my name listed on the scoreboard and announced over the PA system. The team did everything for me except allow me to suit up for the game. I was virtually an honorary member of the team.

If we are in Christ, we have been blessed far beyond the forgiveness we have in Him. God has done far more than declare us to be not guilty. He has adopted us into His family: "Behold what manner of love the Father has bestowed on us, that we should be called children of God!" (1 John 3:1).

One could argue that this is the kind of thing John has in mind here, that we are allowed to be *called* children of God. In other words, we're not really His children, but because of the covenant of grace, we are allowed to use the term.

This word *covenant* is an important one, one that we are often too quick to define, and therefore often define badly. We think *covenant* is simply a fancy word for *contract*. To be certain there are important overlaps between *contract* and *covenant*. Both involve requirements and stipulations. Both involve promises and warnings. But there is a critical difference. The concept of contract is a legal one, but the concept of covenant is relational. That is, when I married my dear wife, we agreed to measurable responsibilities. I endowed her with all my earthly goods, and she did the same for me. We promised to forsake all others till death do us part. But our relationship is much more than merely legal.

When I come home from a business trip, my wife does not hand me a bill. She doesn't charge me for the work she does in caring for the children, cooking meals, etc. I don't counter her bill with one from me in which I subtract from her bill all the money I contribute for the roof over our heads or the groceries. Instead we greet one another with a kiss and a hug, joyful to be together.

The same is true with respect to the gospel. We tend to reduce it to its contractual elements, considering the work of Christ in terms of a financial transaction. We speak of our sins as being credited to Jesus' account, and His righteousness being credited to ours. This is true, and helpful in its place, but it is only part of the truth. When we adopt this view of the gospel, I suspect we imagine a future something like this: we think that when we die we will stand in a long line waiting for our time before God, our judge. When our name is finally called, God looks down at us from on high and asks us how we plead. Because we understand the work of Christ, we plead not guilty because of the blood of Christ shed on our behalf. God then looks over His papers, perhaps checking His book to see if our name is listed there, and finally pounds His gavel and declares, "Not guilty. Next . . ." We then sheepishly make our way around His desk, looking for the pearly gates to slip through.

The only part of this story that fits with what the Bible describes is that God is indeed wearing a robe. He is not, however, sitting behind a desk. According to the Bible, what the gospel tells us is not that we wait in line to see God but He waits, looking off into the distance for us. He takes His robe and binds it up so His legs might enjoy greater freedom of motion as He runs to meet us. When He does meet us, He throws His arms around us, weeping and rejoicing:

> When [the son] was still a great way off, his father saw him and had compassion, and ran and fell on his neck and kissed him. And the son said to him, "Father, I have sinned against heaven and in your sight, and am no longer worthy to be called your son."
>
> But the father said to his servants, "Bring out the best robe and put it on him, and put a ring on his hand and sandals on his feet. And bring the fatted calf here and kill it, and let us eat and be merry; for this my son was dead and is alive again; he was lost and is found." And they began to be merry.
>
> LUKE 15:20-24

This is far more than mere forgiveness. This is a glorious reunion of a father and a son.

First John, however, does not merely tell us that we are the children of God. The good news is not just about the name above ours on our birth certificate. Instead the glorious truth that we are His children is given as evidence of this glorious truth: He loves us! What may well be the greatest hindrance to adults living as children is that we fail to believe that God actually loves us as His children. If we believed that He loved us, we would not spend our days striving to gain acclaim and approval and wrestling with others for honor and position.

What the gospel tells us is not that we wait in line to see God but He waits, looking off into the distance for us. He takes His robe and binds it up so His legs might enjoy greater freedom of motion as He runs to meet us.

Children, all things being equal, are confident of the love they have from their fathers. Indeed they rest in that. So should we. So since we are His children, we are called to remember, to rejoice, to rest in His love for us. When God calls me to travel from time to time, I have a certain routine that I follow with my own children. I hug them, I kiss them, and I give them these instructions: be a help to Mommy, remember that Daddy misses you, and remember that Daddy loves you.

Our Father in heaven, of course, never leaves us, so we need no such instructions. But we should remember this glorious truth each morning when we wake and every night as we go to bed. Our Father in heaven *loves us* with an unchangeable, eternal, and infinite love. That is good news.

First John 3, however, doesn't end with our being the beloved children of the Father. It instead looks to the same future that we anticipate with hope. We are told not only what we are, but what we will be. A day is coming when we will be like our elder Brother, Jesus, the firstborn of many brethren (see v. 2).

When I won that contest as a boy, it was one of the

happiest days of my life. I was going to be given the opportunity not just to watch my heroes at work, but to meet them, to spend time with them. It is because we are blasé adults rather than excitable children that we have to be coaxed here to grasp the fullness, the giddy joyfulness of what is being promised. We are not promised that we will be honorary members of the family of God. We are not promised that we will be made benchwarmers on the greatest team. We are promised that we will be *like Him*, that we are being made into our Hero!

As children, we have an innate, immediate grasp of the great gap that separates us from the glory that is Christ. This gap moves us to awe, to trust, to wonder. This gap moves us to seek to please Him. But the gap itself is actually closed by the gospel. Our Hero's great work is that He is making us into heroes. Our elder Brother's great project for us, who are now only children, is that we become mature. We are in the process of growing up. But as we grow, we don't turn and despise our youth. Instead we rejoice in it, knowing with the trust of a child that His plan is the best plan. We don't mourn the loss of innocence, because by His grace we are moving into greater innocence as He cuts away from us all that is displeasing in His sight.

John finally makes a connection that most of us breeze right past. We know that we are sinners. We understand the importance of understanding and believing the promises of God. We begin to scratch the surface of the gospel truth that we are His children, that He loves us and will love us forever.

We step further into joy as we remember that in His love for us He is giving us the greatest gift He could possibly give—He is making us more like His precious Son.

We will become more like children as we gain a greater understanding of what it means that we are indeed His children. He has rescued us. He loves us. He has adopted us as His own. He has made us heirs of the Kingdom. He has promised to raise us up in the way that we should go so that we will not depart from it. And He has promised to make us like Him. How can we not be confident of the love of such a Father? As we grow into greater childlikeness, we will find increasing joy in pleasing Him and knowing we are the recipients of His smile.

7

THE CALL TO MATURITY

Do not be children in understanding; however, in malice be babes, but in understanding be mature.

1 CORINTHIANS 14:20

IT WAS A STRANGE, providential confluence that so many heroes should descend on my fair city on the same day. I was a first-year student at Reformed Theological Seminary during its first year in Orlando. That same fall another institution began in Orlando, the Orlando Magic NBA basketball team. I cheered for the Magic, of course, but my heart remained loyal to the team I had cheered for from my youth, the basketball equivalent of the Pittsburgh Steelers, the Boston Celtics.

The Celtics were scheduled to come to Orlando only once that first year, and in God's grace, I had not only a ticket to the game but a seat on the floor. The championship team from the 1980s was still mostly intact. I would see Robert Parish, Dennis Johnson, Danny Ainge, Kevin McHale, and Larry Bird, up close and personal.

The day of the game, however, was the first day of a week-long January class at seminary, meeting each day from eight until five. We were studying Jonathan Edwards, one of my theological heroes. The professor who would be teaching us, Dr. John Gerstner, was a hero not only to me but to my greater hero, my father. So there I was that Monday morning, in a class being taught by my hero, who is also my hero's hero, studying together his hero as I waited to go see my basketball heroes play.

I didn't hear much that first day of class. As excited as I was to be studying with Dr. Gerstner, I was somewhat distracted. There were eight students in the class and we began going over our assignments. Dr. Gerstner explained that each of us would be given a portion of Edwards's work *The Freedom of the Will.* We would be required to give a forty-five-minute presentation and then answer questions for forty-five minutes. There are four parts to the Edwards essay. That all sounded wonderful, until Dr. Gerstner said that I would be giving my report on the first fourth of the essay the next morning. That's when I stopped listening.

The remaining hours of class I spent wrestling over this seemingly impossible choice. I could go to the one game I had been looking forward to all season long and do a miserable job on my assignment. Or I could put aside my objectively petty desires and apply myself to my real calling as a student. I could please my hero who was also my father's hero, and in so doing, please my father. Or I could watch Larry Bird.

Back and forth I went until class ended at five. I got in my car and drove straight to the arena. I had finally made up my mind. I was going to do both, whatever it might take. I would go to the game, enjoy it, soak it in. I would likely get home around eleven, and if I needed to stay up until five in the morning, I would do it. I would go to class, give my report, fight to stay awake the rest of the day, and recover later. I was determined to burn the candle at both ends, play both sides against the middle. I would tap into the same youth that led me to make the wrong decision to find the stamina to cover my folly.

Which is precisely what I did. I don't honestly remember much about the game. I don't remember a great deal about my presentation. I remember even less what was said the rest of that long day. I know my presentation garnered a compliment I don't think I'll ever forget—Dr. Gerstner told my father, who had been his student about thirty years earlier, "It was like watching you all over again."

Despite those encouraging words, and despite still feeling the pain of the choice I had before me that day, I look back on my decision with regret. I wasn't torn because I had such a hard time discerning what the right choice was. I was torn because the right choice and the choice I really wanted to make were opposites. The fact that I managed to cover for myself the day following the game doesn't change that I chose "want" over "ought." I hope I have learned and grown since then and that if I were given such a choice again, I would behave with greater maturity and do the right thing.

When we started looking at our call to be like children, we recognized what, on the surface, an odd command this was from our Maker. We serve the God of surprises, and His perspective is always correct and will always correct us where ours is wrong. We also noted, however, that the devil's delight is not only to encourage us to miss or disdain this calling but to cause us to race in the opposite direction. His will is that we will embrace those aspects of youth that we should be outgrowing and putting behind us and will reject those aspects we are called to. Our enemy not only wants us to be "mature" in the worst possible ways, but also wants us to flee the proper biblical call to maturity. He wants us to have it wrong on every account.

In the beginning of the book, I suggested that while the bulk of our attention would be focused on what it looks like to become more like children in the biblical sense, we would also take some time to consider our calling to mature. The New Testament has plenty of calls to maturity, to completeness. If we would be like children, eager to please, trusting, we would also have a desire to become more mature.

Paul makes one such call to maturity in a context that highlights our abiding call to still be like children. He writes: "Brethren, do not be children in understanding; however, in malice be babes, but in understanding be mature" (1 Corinthians 14:20). If ever a church struggled with both an unbecoming lack of maturity and a deep need to become more like children, it was the church at Corinth. This church was rocked with schism and scandal, all rooted in pride. Paul had to deal with the Apollos-ites, the Peter-ites, even the Paul-ites, groups of purported Christians who defined their identity not in terms of following Christ but in following a favorite teacher. In addition, the Corinthians thought themselves so mature, so committed to grace, that they countenanced a man having his father's wife—something, Paul rightly points out, even the unbelievers would never do.

That same spirit showed itself in a prideful pursuit of spiritual gifts in that church. Too many people saw the gifts as signs of the spiritual superiority of those who had them. In chapter 13, Paul reminds the Corinthians that none of the things they are scrambling for mean anything without love. In 14:20, he calls them not to be children in understanding, which may well be the beginning of what maturity looks like. I'm afraid, however, that I am still tempted to be sufficiently immature that I confuse maturity of understanding with a willingness and ability to bicker over fine points of theology. Is that what Paul is getting at here?

I don't think so. To be mature in understanding is not ultimately about knowing the definitions and nuances of complex theological concepts. To be mature in our thinking is not related to whether we read the most provocative theologians of our day. Ironically, maturity of understanding may well be remembering, and resting in, the simplest things.

Of course we should give thanks for our fathers in the

faith who have helped us come to understand deep theological issues in light of the Word. At the same time, we need to be mature enough to confess that the gospel is simple enough that even a child can understand. Think of Philip's encounter with the Ethiopian eunuch. Although the eunuch was already studying the wisdom of Isaiah, his embrace of the finished work of Christ surely came before Philip could give a lecture on propitiation. The thief on the cross had studied very little and had even less explained to him, but he was assured by Jesus Himself of a place in paradise. We should never equate theological snobbery with spiritual maturity.

That maturity is measured less by being able to quote the best rabbis and more by being steady, by not being "tossed and blown about by every wind of new teaching" (Ephesians 4:14, NLT). In the church where I served, we had a young man who was an avid student of theology. He had come from a challenging background and was not well educated, but his passion led him to read widely and, by and large, wisely. At church events he liked nothing better than to sit and discuss all he was learning. He was a likable fellow as well, and so it came to pass that he not only tended to pontificate but also found himself with a decent-sized group of followers who were eager to learn from him.

Everything was going okay until he began to explore an obscure and dangerous position on end-times theology. He had been doing some reading on a view that holds that every biblical prophecy has already come to pass, that we have nothing more to look forward to. I had done some reading on this view and had written on it as well. What raised my eyebrows, and those of the other elders in the church, was that we heard him wonder out loud to his usual crowd whether maybe there was no future Resurrection to look forward to. Maybe Jesus wasn't coming back after all. Suddenly his studies had led him, and by extension those who were listening to him, right off the true path.

This is precisely the kind of immaturity that Paul is warning against. Because we live in an egalitarian age, we think our own speculations ought to be given the same weight as the wisdom of the centuries. We do not honor the fathers who have gone before us, and we think too highly of ourselves. A mature understanding is a self-aware understanding, one that knows how deceitful our own hearts can be. As one wise theologian once put it, if you have come up with an idea that has been rejected by the church as error for two thousand years, how likely is it that you are correct and the rest of the church throughout history is wrong?

Maturity means, in part, holding to the great truths of Scripture carried down through the ages. It means recognizing that any speculation that takes our eyes off the once-for-all provision of Christ for us is not only wrong but dangerous. It remembers the repeated wisdom of Paul, that when we add anything to Christ's work, we take away Christ's work. As we cling to the truths of Scripture, we see that Word maturing in us and, in the end, bearing much fruit.

Note, too, that with respect to malice, Paul brings together maturity of thought with childlikeness. We don't lose one to gain the other. Instead, the two are tied tightly together. When we remember that we are children who were rescued, not theological geniuses who scaled the heights of sound thinking on our own, we remove malice from our hearts. We do not engage in competition to demonstrate who of us is the smartest, because we remember that "smart" is not an attribute of the fruit of the Spirit.

Paul, who I believe wrote the book of Hebrews, does much the same in a familiar passage:

> Though by this time you ought to be teachers, you need someone to teach you again the first principles of the oracles of God; and you have come to need milk and not solid food. For everyone who partakes only of milk is unskilled in the word of righteousness, for he is a babe. But solid food belongs to those who are of full age, that is, those who by reason of use have their senses exercised to discern both good and evil.
>
> HEBREWS 5:12-14

How sinful I am if I take this warning *against* pride and turn it into an opportunity *for* pride. If I take Paul's wisdom and divide the Kingdom of God into two camps: the poor, ignorant, immature, milk people; and the meat people, people like me. Paul is not criticizing his audience for not becoming sufficiently skilled in talking about deep theology. He does not—and neither should we—measure spiritual maturity by the clarity and insight of our arguments over just how many angels can pirouette on the head of a pin. The solid food we are called to here is related to our ability to discern between good and evil.

In my own tradition we miss the force of what Paul is saying here precisely because we don't understand. We think that the good and evil we are called to discern is good theological precision and evil theological error. That is, because we measure our level of spiritual maturity not by how godly we are but by how much we know, we measure good and evil in the same way. We think Paul is urging the rest of the church to become more like us—theologically puffed up, proud, self-righteous. But what Paul is saying is precisely the opposite. We demonstrate our spiritual maturity as we recognize that we ourselves are but babes. We chew on the meat of the Word when we meditate on what it means to fulfill our calling to be like children.

We should not measure spiritual maturity by the clarity and insight of our arguments over just how many angels can pirouette on the head of a pin, but rather by whether we are able to discern between good and evil.

How do we know this? Paul tells us. Remember that the Bible's chapter and verse divisions were not inspired by the Holy Spirit. They are a human invention that often helps and occasionally obscures. As Hebrews 5 ends and chapter 6 begins, Paul does not leave off discussing milk and meat and take up something new. Instead, he expands and expounds on his point:

> Leaving the discussion of the elementary principles of Christ, let us go on to perfection [completeness or maturity], not laying again the foundation of repentance from dead works and of faith toward God, of the doctrine of baptisms, of laying on of hands, of resurrection of the dead, and of eternal judgment. And this we will do if God permits.
>
> HEBREWS 6:1-3

Remember that these are the basics that we are to master before moving on to the meat. What we are supposed to master is repentance from dead works and faith toward God. The basic things are not the person and work of Christ and justification, while the meaty things are predestination and providence. Rather, these basics all center on our relationship with our heavenly Father. Do we recognize our dependence? Do we believe what our Father is telling us, giving Him our "amen" to whatever He speaks? Do we believe His promises in His covenants and the promise of the world to come, when we will be like Him because we will see Him as He is? We can't move on to the meat until we have mastered these things and have attained a most basic level of maturity. We have to learn to discern good and evil. That's what maturity looks like, what Adam and Eve grasped for before they were ready. So if we are called to this maturity, where do we find it?

Remembering that James and Paul believed the same gospel and served the same Lord (just like Apollos, Peter, and Paul, which the Corinthians failed to understand), let's see whether James might give us some wisdom on where and how to attain spiritual maturity. If anyone could have laid claim to the title of "mature" among all the saints in the New Testament, James would be the one. According to most scholars, the epistle of James was the first New Testament letter written. Despite his denial of Christ when he was younger, James, the half-brother of Jesus, became not just a believer but a great leader in the early church. He presided over the Jerusalem counsel that was called to deal with the circumcision question (see Acts 15). And tradition says that he earned the nickname Camel Knees because he spent so much time in prayer that his knees became misshapen, like those of a camel. He was, in short, a father to the faithful.

In James's letter, having affirmed his status as a mere servant of God and Jesus Christ, he quickly shows us the path to maturity:

> My brethren, count it all joy when you fall into various trials, knowing that the testing of your faith produces patience. But let patience have its perfect work, that you may be perfect and complete, lacking nothing.
>
> JAMES 1:2-4

That path to spiritual maturity, says James, is trials. The sign that we are on the path, however, is that we rejoice even in the midst of those trials. James is no philosophical stoic, calling on us to exert the will to keep a stiff upper lip. He isn't merely calling us to endure, to persevere, in light of all that God has already done for us. He isn't asking us to practice a kind of mind-over-matter principle. Rather, we can and should consider it a reason for joy when trials and difficulties come our way because they test our faith, and that testing produces patience. We count it all joy because in the end, that patience results in its perfect work, making us complete, lacking nothing—in other words, *mature*.

Maturity, in short, is the ability to discern good and evil, because it knows what the greatest good is. We are immature when we think God has put us on the planet so that we might enjoy comfort and ease. We are mature when we understand that the greatest gift we could be given is that we might be more like Him. Comfort and ease make us fat and temporarily happy. On the other hand, trials mature us, making us more like Him: fit and holy.

Several years ago my dear wife and I found ourselves going through a long string of hardships. She was diagnosed with breast cancer the day before I lost a job I had hoped to have my whole life. Our daughter Shannon started suffering horrible seizures. There were broken relationships in our church. We were dealing with literally one thing after another, but God sustained us during that time. And as we began to see some light at the end of the tunnel (a temporary reprieve, to be sure, as we continue to face these same kinds of challenges years later), I confessed to Denise that I thought I knew why all this was happening: it was because of something I did.

"What did you do?" she asked.

"Well, it's something I said, in a manner of speaking."

"What did you say?" she asked.

"Well, it was something I prayed."

Denise's voice climbed still higher as she asked, "What did you pray?"

I had prayed something like this:

Lord, You know my heart so much better than I do. You know the depth and the scope of my sin, and I thank You that You only allow me to see more of it slowly. Even so, I know something of what my heart longs for. I want comfort. I want ease. I want to be respected and honored. My heart longs for prosperity. Lord, I want all the things that I know I'm not supposed to want. By Your grace my mind at least knows what I am supposed to want, even though my heart is reluctant to follow. So please hear my prayer. I want You to please pay no attention whatever to the desires of my heart. Ignore them. Lord, when I complain bitterly to You that You are not giving me what I long for, turn a deaf ear to me. My prayer, Lord, is that You would hear the prayer of my mind, not the prayer of my heart. Please, O Lord, hear this. My prayer is that You would be pleased to make me more like Your Son Jesus. Lord, I'm pleading with You to please send whatever it takes. Whatever it takes. *And, Lord, please do the same for my beloved bride and for the children You have given us.*

The same joy that James calls us to with respect to our trials is what Jesus calls us to rejoice over. Only twice in the New Testament are God's people called to rejoice and be exceedingly glad. The first time is in the Sermon on the Mount. There, after promising us blessing when we hunger and thirst for righteousness, when we are meek, when we are peacemakers, when we mourn, when we are poor in spirit, He tells us what will make us "exceedingly glad": "Blessed are you when they revile and persecute you, and say all kinds of evil against you falsely for My sake. Rejoice and be exceedingly glad, *for great is your reward in heaven*, for so they persecuted the prophets who were before you" (Matthew 5:11-12, emphasis added). The promise of Jesus is that as we go through persecution for His name's sake, we can know for certain that we will receive a great reward in heaven. Indeed, at least part of that great reward is that we will be made like Him. And the more like Him we are made, even while we are here on earth, the more we experience heaven on this side of eternity.

On this point, Jesus may well be pointing to one of the defining qualities of maturity—the ability to delay gratification. Recently I came face-to-face with that issue. It is my habit each morning to walk about three and a half miles, in large part because I'm not so mature in my eating choices. I would rather wake while it is dark and walk around in circles than give up the gratification I get from eating french fries. Recently I have been taking my youngest son, Donovan, with me. Donovan, almost two years old as I was writing this, enjoys the ride in the jogging stroller. He may well be the only one in the family who wakes before me. He has been told to stay in his crib until someone comes to get him, but he has learned to scale the side and escape. So when he wakes, he is faced with a choice, and that choice provides an opportunity to teach him through consequences.

When I go to his room and find him in his crib, I get him up, change and dress him, and off we go on our walk. If I find him playing on the floor, he is merely put back in the crib, and I go off alone. His choices are clear: he can get out of bed earlier and explore his room, or he can wait and explore the great outdoors with me. He can see the flock of turkeys that lives in our neighborhood, countless squirrels, or even the dozen deer that graze there each morning. When he is able to delay gratification, his gratification is much fuller.

I try to live by the same principle and to instill it in all my children. The simple mantra in our house is "work now, play later." Sometimes I can even apply the principle to a fault. If you came to our house for supper, you would likely wonder what happened to me after the meal. I can't seem to bring myself to sit down and visit, even with close friends, when I know that there are dirty dishes in the kitchen. Work now, play later—I do the dishes first.

Maturity, in turn, is the fruit of seeing with the eyes of faith. Children gasp and cheer over magic tricks precisely because they believe what their eyes see. Ultimately, however, God calls us to believe not what we see but what God says. Mature people look at what they see, at their circumstances, and stand firm on the promises of God. They have the capacity to remember history, to hold on to all those times when God delivered His people. Those who are mature look both backward and forward: back to God's faithfulness and deliverances in the past, and forward to His promises yet to unfold.

When Paul was writing to the Corinthians, he was facing a common malady: the erosion of faith that can come from the pain of suffering:

> We have this treasure in earthen vessels, that the excellence of the power may be of God and not of us. We are hard-pressed on every side, yet not crushed; we are perplexed, but not in despair; persecuted, but not forsaken; struck down, but not destroyed—always carrying about in the body the dying of the Lord Jesus, that the life of Jesus also may be manifested in our body. For we who live are always delivered to death for Jesus' sake, that the life of Jesus also may be manifested in our mortal flesh. So then death is working in us, but life in you.
>
> And since we have the same spirit of faith, according to what is written, "*I believed and therefore I spoke,*" we also believe and therefore speak, knowing that He who raised up the Lord Jesus will also raise us up with Jesus, and will present us with you. For all things are for your sakes, that grace, having spread through the many, may cause thanksgiving to abound to the glory of God. Therefore we do not lose heart.
>
> 2 CORINTHIANS 4:7-16 (EMPHASIS ADDED)

Those who are mature experience all those hardships—being hard-pressed, perplexed, persecuted, struck down—but they manage to not be crushed, not be in despair, knowing God has not forsaken them. The mature know and see the invisible but unbreakable connection between their own suffering and that of our Lord. Better still, they know and see the invisible and unbreakable connection between the suffering and dying of our Lord and His and our resurrection. Children sometimes throw tantrums when we don't allow them to have their own way. Those who are mature, however, are patient and wise and know the good that will come from the hardships they suffer.

When we are mature, we are able to make careful, rational comparisons between today's hardship and tomorrow's promises. As we do this, we see not that the scales will balance in the end or that we will come out a little to the good. Instead, that sober comparison ends with a childlike fit of the giggles as we see the overflowing abundance of the grace promised to us. So Paul continues: "Even though our outward man is perishing, yet the inward man is being renewed day by day. For our light affliction, which is but for a moment, is working for us a far more exceeding and eternal weight of glory, while we do not look at the things which are seen, but at the things which are not seen. For the things which are seen are temporary, but the things which are not seen are eternal" (2 Corinthians 4:16-18).

Because we are childish, not childlike, we end up missing the fullness of the gospel. C. S. Lewis makes this point in *The Weight of Glory*:

> Indeed, if we consider the unblushing promises of reward and the staggering nature of the rewards promised in the Gospels, it would seem that Our Lord finds our desires, not too strong, but too weak. We are half-hearted creatures, fooling about with drink and sex and ambition when infinite joy is offered us, like an ignorant child who wants to go on making mud pies in a slum because he cannot imagine what is meant by the offer of a holiday at the sea. We are far too easily pleased.

The maturity to know and to believe all that God has promised us leads to a reaction akin to a child's on Christmas morning. But we are guilty of worshiping the god of our age, the god the late Francis Schaeffer dubbed "the idol of personal peace and affluence." This god, however, is as worthless, as unable to fulfill, as drink, sex, and ambition.

Because we are more adult than actually mature, we tend to take our sins and baptize them, dressing them up as spiritual maturity. One temptation I have had to fight over and over is confusing my own level of knowledge with spiritual maturity. Not content to sinfully take pride in the scope of my personal library, I sinfully saw it as a sign of spiritual depth. But God helped me with this one evening in an unexpected way. I was a first-year seminary student at a first-year seminary. Because Reformed Theological Seminary had just opened its Orlando campus, there was an understandable push to fill its seats. It offered multiple nighttime classes and advertised in local churches, seeking interested laypeople to come and study. It also sought local pastors who might not already have a graduate-school theological education. The result, in my proud mind, was a watered-down curriculum. Not enough heavy and heady arguments, too many Sunday-school-style lessons.

One particular evening our professor invited a student to open the class in prayer. That was a common enough practice, but this time I was concerned. The professor had asked one of the "uneducated" pastors to pray. In other classes, this man would ask the simplest, most basic questions, things he should have learned as a child. And now he was going to pray for us. I bowed my head, ready to take mental note of every error he expressed, when something astonishing happened—he started speaking to God.

Because we are more adult than actually mature, we tend to take our sins and baptize them, dressing them up as spiritual maturity.

I don't know if I could put my finger on the difference between his prayers and my own. I don't doubt that he spoke an occasional theological error along the way. But as I listened, I knew he was a man who knew God far more intimately than I ever had. I knew that he knew he was with God Most High. I knew he was used to this kind of thing, though he certainly did not take it for granted. Three minutes into the prayer, I had had enough of tracking with him, and I began to pray more earnestly than I ever had before. My prayer went something like this:

O Lord, I know You are sovereign, almighty. I know that You are able to do all Your holy will. I do not doubt Your strength, but I have come today to know so much more about my weakness. I want to ask You for a miracle. Lord, could You, would You be willing, before I die, to make me half the man that man is? Is it even possible that You should so work in me? Lord, because I know You are able, as astonishing as it is, to forgive my arrogance and pride in thinking myself this man's better, could You also make me better than I am?

This is what we are to long for, that as we grow older and mature, we would become less what we were and more what we are called to be. The hunger for maturity is nothing more or less than the desire to be made more like Jesus. He is the express image of the complete person. He is "The Man," as even Pilate recognized (see John 19:5). There is, however, only one path to get there: the Via Dolorosa, the way of suffering. This is how we mature, how we grow in grace and wisdom, how we become spiritual adults and at the same time, how we become like children.

As children we are called to trust, to lean on the Word, on the promises of our Father in heaven. We are not to cynically twist or distort those promises but rather believe them with reckless abandon. We do this by stepping into the blood-stained shoes of our elder Brother and walking the pathway He has blazed for us. The cost is indeed high, but the reward is beyond measure. By God's grace, as we mature, we may hope that on our deathbed we will be able to speak these last words: "I have *fought the good fight*, I have finished the race,

I have kept the faith (2 Timothy 4:7, emphasis added). And when we pass through to the other side, we will be blessed to hear the first words of the rest of the story: "Well done, good and faithful servant! . . . Come and share your master's happiness!" (Matthew 25:21, NIV).

8

THE CALL TO JOY

Rejoice and be exceedingly glad, for great is your reward in heaven.
MATTHEW 5:12

It is a rite in virtually every distinct culture. Humanity, as humanity, seems to sense a need not only to draw a clear line but also to mark and celebrate the crossing of that line. When a boy becomes a man, or a girl becomes a woman, something profound has happened. The Jewish people mark the event with the *bar mitzvah* (or *bat mitzvah* for girls). Some tribes of Native Americans send their boys off on a vision quest and welcome back men. Apache girls spend four days and nights in tests of endurance, strength, and character and are received back as women, ready to take their place in the culture.

A friend of mine came up with his own ceremony. When he deemed that his son had become a man, he invited hundreds of friends over to feast in celebration and marked that milestone not only by giving the son a speech but also by giving him a sword.

The broader American culture, however, is fast losing sight of the importance of marking this shift. Beyond perhaps the bureaucratic rite of registering for the military draft, what ceremony do we have? One could argue that we have no ceremony because we have no earthly idea when to have it. Immaturity is running so rampant among the young people of our land that the epidemic even has a name—failure to launch. Even when a young man succeeds in leaving the nest and establishing a home, there is still another hurdle to get over: the boomerang effect. In record numbers we are seeing young people either failing to leave their parents' homes or returning to those homes.

Though I had established my own home several years earlier, I did go through what might these days pass for a ceremony recognizing my entering adulthood. I was already a blessed husband and a grateful father of two young children. Denise and I had, in God's good grace, been given a complete set, first a little girl and then a little boy. At this point, conventional wisdom would have encouraged us to head for the next stage of our lives and put childbearing behind us. But we took the view that children are a blessing from the hand of God (Psalm 127) and sought to be blessed still more. God heard our prayers, and so, with a three-year-old daughter and a one-year-old son, we found ourselves expecting again.

The arrival of our third child wasn't by itself the change I went through—it just precipitated the change. When Denise and I were first married, we each brought into our lives together various assets. I brought a BMW. It was well used when I bought it, and by the time we had been married for four years, its odometer had passed 150,000 and was nearing 200,000. It was also prompting frequent and expensive trips to the repair shop. A few years earlier I had bought my wife a nice, safe, also-well-used Volvo station wagon with only half as many miles as my car. Here is where my sweet wife broached the subject. Though we certainly could squeeze three children in their car seats into the back of the Volvo, she thought it wiser at that point to do the grown-up thing and buy a minivan.

The moment had come. I had three choices before me. I could have failed the test miserably and insisted that I would not trade in the Volvo on a minivan, arguing that I was both too cool and too young to own such a vehicle. Or I could have passed the test and traded in the Volvo for the minivan. Then I would know that I had done the right thing (and would still get to drive my BMW). The third choice, however, was the A+ option, the one that was above and beyond the call. And I made that call. I agreed not only to get the minivan but also to trade in my BMW for it, leaving me with a Volvo station wagon to drive. Though he was not there to do so, I suspect my father would have proudly intoned, "My son, today you are a man."

Within a matter of months I was over my sacrifice because I had something even better to celebrate. Denise gave birth to our third child, blessing number three. Shannon was something of a butterball, but she scored well on the Apgar index. For the first time we had a baby who didn't suffer a strong case of jaundice, and she learned fairly quickly how to sleep through the night without ever taking a ride on the dryer. Darby and Campbell rejoiced to have a new little sister. Darby was once asked during the pregnancy if she hoped it would be a boy or a girl. Darby knew not only what she wanted but why, replying, "Mommy and Daddy and I already have a little boy."

When Shannon was about six months old, we began to notice some very small issues with her. She wasn't hitting all the typical benchmarks in her abilities. There were slight tremors in her arms at times. She was somewhat cross-eyed. And she wasn't gaining weight. Our wonderful family doctor gave us counsel on this issue and that. Shannon saw a specialist and had surgery to fix her eye. We started pouring liquid butter into her baby food, hoping it would help her gain weight. We weren't terribly worried.

Then, at the same time Shannon wasn't gaining weight, my dear wife was. After three children, all born roughly two years apart, we were surprised to find ourselves expecting blessing number four a week or so before Shannon's first birthday. We welcomed Delaney into our family just as our concerns over Shannon began to grow. Within two months of Delaney's birth we headed halfway across the state for a multiple-day investigative visit to the University of Virginia Children's Hospital in Charlottesville.

Shannon was seen by multiple specialists while Denise tried her best to care for our newborn. The doctors were concerned but had no explanation for Shannon's symptoms. Just as my mother-in-law was arriving to help Denise so I could return home for a church event, the doctors sent Shannon in for an MRI. It was about midnight that same night, and I had just finished cleaning up the yard after our annual churchwide bonfire, when I heard the crunch of tires on our driveway. My mother-in-law was able to put both Shannon and Delaney into their cribs while my bride, through tears, explained what the doctors had found.

Shannon was diagnosed with *lissencephaly*, which means literally "smooth brain." The MRI showed that Shannon's brain did not have the ridges that most brains have. There are a number of subcategories for this condition, my wife explained, but they didn't know which of those Shannon might fall into. Her prognosis was not good. Most children with lissencephaly, Denise had been told, spend their short lives lying in cribs, connected to feeding tubes and fighting off seizures until death finally takes them.

I felt myself being helplessly squeezed. As a husband I wanted nothing more than to be able to heal the heartbreak of my wife. As a father I wanted nothing more than to be able to comfort and heal my daughter. As a man I grieved that I was so utterly helpless. There was nothing I could do except hold my wife as we cried together into that dark night.

The next morning there were more conversations. We spoke with our family doctor. We spoke with the elders of our church. We spoke with each other. And then we called my parents. I managed to fight back the tears long enough to give all the information we had. My parents both spoke tenderly to me. I could hear their own pain in their voices. Finally, my father asked me, "Son, how are you doing? How are you handling this?"

As a husband I wanted nothing more than to be able to heal the heartbreak of my wife. As a father I wanted nothing more than to be able to comfort and heal my daughter. As a man I grieved that I was so utterly helpless. There was nothing I could do except hold my wife as we cried together into that dark night.

I smiled at the irony and answered him. "Dad," I said, "I have been preparing for this moment my entire life. There is no faith on the planet that more strongly affirms the sovereignty of God than the Christian faith. We know this did not catch God by surprise. We know that Shannon, Denise, and I all rest in His loving hands. We will, by His grace and in His power, be able to manage."

I hung up the phone thinking myself quite the theologically sound fellow for seeing the hand of Providence in all this and for believing God would bless us with the strength to endure. And as is always the case when I think well of myself, I could not have been more wrong. God did not sustain me and my family in the midst of this great hardship. It was not even true that He had ordained such a hard providence. What we came to discover was something far more profound, something far more astonishing, far more gospel infused.

Shannon, just like Darby, Campbell, Delaney, and all the children who would come later, was, as He had promised, a profound blessing, a gift, a source of immeasurable joy. Neither Shannon nor her illness was a burden to be carried; they are a blessing to be received. The God of surprises, not being a tame lion, showered us with His love, in and through His servant Shannon.

It is true enough that our lives became more complicated than we might have expected. We read all that we could find on this strange condition. We had more testing done. Therapists came to help out. Shannon did begin to slowly pick up a few skills, though always late. She began to crawl. She began to reach out and grasp the toys she wanted to play with. She began to be able to pick up raisins with her own fingers. She learned to hold her own bottle.

We began to notice a marked gap between what we were told to expect and what she was able to do. We called her the "world champion lissencephalic child." She showed signs of understanding us, smiling when we asked, "Would you like your bottle?" Around the time she turned two, she even began to make some guttural sounds, which were often intermingled with her frequent fits of laughter. We worked with her, took her to experts, gave her dietary supplements.

There were, of course, moments of sadness. It was hard to watch Shannon's younger sister pass her up in abilities. Two years later, Erin Claire was born, and eighteen months after that we were blessed with Maili. With each child we would watch this marvelous shift in relationship. Shannon was interested in but terribly protective of the little babies God sent into our family. As the babies grew into toddlers, Shannon welcomed them as peers, playing with them, sharing with them. And as the toddlers became little children, Shannon began to look to them for protection, for help. We would reflect on and mourn the hard truth that she would never marry, that she would likely never make a verbal profession of faith in Christ and partake of the elements in the Lord's Supper.

Given, however, that we as a family are so passionate about the blessing of little babies, how great was it that we would have this little baby with us for years and years? About the time Shannon turned four, we estimated that her abilities were roughly those of a two-year-old. And then it happened. She was in her crib, laughing and jumping, when I came into her room. She shouted out, as clear as a bell, "Eeyadee!!" I don't pretend to know for certain. I surely couldn't prove it in court. But my heart knew—she had just called me Daddy.

She managed to squeal that little miracle a few more times in the coming year. If food was sufficiently sticky, like oatmeal, she learned to get a few spoonfuls into her mouth. We continued to rejoice in her progress and to revel in her joy. She earned her nickname, Princess Happy. Our research showed that much of the hardship, much of the challenge, lissencephalic children dealt with was the result of seizures. We learned also that lissencephalic children who made it to five years of age without seizures were unlikely to develop them.

It was Resurrection Sunday, just a few months after Shannon's fifth birthday. Our family had planned to spend the afternoon with friends, and we were getting ready to head out the door. Shannon was in her room when she suddenly fainted. In the middle of taking a step as she crossed the room, her entire body instantly went limp. She collapsed like a rag doll and lay still exactly where she landed. I picked her up and held her, relieved at least to be able to feel her breathing. I spoke to her, trying to rouse her, but to no avail. Denise called the doctor, who confirmed what we feared: a seizure. What a strange providence, that on the day when we celebrate our Lord's victory over death, we had a potent reminder that death still haunted our home.

Shannon was put on seizure medicine that seemed at least to hold back the tide. She continued to suffer from the tiniest little "drop" seizures, often going limp in midstride but recovering before her foot hit the ground. The more dramatic ones were somewhat rare. We entered into a new normal and gave thanks once again to have her in our family.

A father feels protective of his children. That protective instinct will heat up, especially for daughters. But never is it stronger than with a frail and needy daughter. Of course, my dear wife cared for and watched over Shannon. And Shannon's siblings have been from the beginning the very models of compassion and giving. As new babies were welcomed into our house and Shannon grew bigger and heavier, much of her care, to my joy, fell to me. I get to feed her most of her meals. I am blessed to be able to give her her baths.

That blessed time together, along with the first real brush with the reality that she wouldn't always be with us, finally broke through my ignorance and pride. In the providence of God we had planned a family trip to Knoxville, Tennessee, two hours from our home. Shannon had an appointment with a specialist at the children's hospital there, and the rest of the family planned to visit family friends. We were about ten minutes from the hospital when Shannon suddenly began to shake in her chair. Her body clenched, and she began to vomit violently. Her eyes were rolling into the back of her head. I could think of nothing to do but hurry. By the time we pulled up to the hospital, the seizure and vomiting had ended, but Shannon's whole body was shivering. I swept her out of the van and held her close right on the sidewalk, rocking her back and forth as my own tears mingled with my prayers, *Please Lord, not now. Not yet. Please don't take her from us. We need her.*

Shannon survived and needed only a slight change in her medications. But at that moment I came to understand the key to the real hardship. Caring for Shannon is a joy. Simply being with her is a joy. The credit others give my wife and me for our faith or our selflessness is literally laughable. Shannon isn't a hardship to be endured; she's a blessing to be enjoyed. There is, however, one hardship. It isn't that now, at fourteen, she still needs to have her diaper changed. It isn't the expense of the medications and the experts. The hardship isn't even specifically watching her suffer through a seizure. Rather, the hardship is what the seizure reminds us at such a gut level:

Shannon is almost certainly going to go home to her reward before the rest of us.

The measure of her days, I realized that day on the sidewalk, isn't determined by her frailty. We don't chart her decline and calculate how soon she is likely to leave. Instead I came to understand that our Lord, our heavenly Father, would call her home when Shannon was done with us. She is a gift and a joy. Her greatest gift, however, is what she teaches us. She is less a weaker person whom I must tend to and more a hero I am called to emulate. Shannon is my spiritual better. I don't long for her to acquire this skill or reach that benchmark. Instead, she is precisely what I want to be when I grow up.

Shannon provides a daily, potent reminder of what it is we are all called to. She is the child Jesus takes into His arms to serve as our example. She is the very picture of trust. Her gait is unsteady, but I need only to show her my hand and she takes it, looking at me with faith and then looking ahead, ready and eager to walk wherever I might lead. Her trust in me, however, far exceeds merely taking a walk. It is not at all uncommon that where I am leading her is a place she might rather not be. Through countless medical procedures, through shots and blood draws, she goes where I take her. She does so without fear, not because she feels no pain but because she trusts me. Somehow, some way, she knows that if I am with her, then what she is going through will be for her good, no matter how much it might hurt her.

Do I trust my heavenly Father as faithfully? Am I ready

to follow Him wherever He might lead? Do I have the confidence that He is always with me and that everything He brings into my life will be for my good? The lesson isn't merely that Shannon trusts her earthly father more than I trust my heavenly Father. The lesson is that she trusts her weak, sinful father more than I trust my omnipotent, holy Father. She has every reason to doubt me. I, on the other hand, have no reason whatsoever to doubt my Father. When she takes my hand, when we begin to walk together, she is speaking to me—gently, lovingly rebuking me without words. *I trust you, Daddy. Can you not trust our heavenly Father?*

Shannon, unlike her siblings, is not able to race to greet me when I come home from work. She is not able to show me the pictures she's drawn or the toad she has managed to capture. She is not able to tell me about the perfect score she received on her math test. However, she is still all too eager to please, as all children are. I know this in large part because of the escalating smiles. She and I repeat this pattern almost every day. When I come to get her up in the morning, or when I bring her the supper that I will feed her, when one way or another we are brought together, we tend to have this wonderful exchange. "Shannon," I say, "Daddy is here. Are you ready for some supper?" Shannon sees my smile and breathes an almost snort through her nose before grinning back at me. It's a sly grin, like we're sharing a secret together. Of course, that widens my own grin. Seeing my smile expand, Shannon next shows all her teeth, and her eyes virtually disappear as her smile envelops her whole face.

Here, too, it is all too easy to see what pleases her, and it is pleasing me. Her delight is to inspire a smile in me and then cause it to grow. She knows what she means to me, which in turn pleases her. I don't for a moment doubt her desire to make me happy. I am in constant doubt, on the other hand, over my level of passion for pleasing my heavenly Father. Do I delight in giving Him delight? Is my pleasure His pleasure? Do we ever share together these escalating smiles? As with the trust issue, Shannon has far less reason to seek to please me than I have to please God. Her father is a sinner. My Father in heaven is perfect. Despite His perfections, however, He delights in a decidedly imperfect me. Here again, Shannon is my spiritual better, my teacher, my model.

Since I cannot be with her always, happily I am not by any stretch the only cause of Shannon's delight. She is nicknamed Princess Happy because she doesn't need a particular excuse for joy. Indeed her joy flows directly out of her constant sense of wonder. We who are older have grown jaded. Our eyes miss the everyday miracles going on all around us. Shannon lives in a constant state of wonder because she receives the grace and beauty of God for what they are and sees them wherever they are—which is everywhere.

Until recently, when her size and seizures made it problematic, it was my habit to take Shannon grocery shopping with me. Grocery shopping is one of the tasks I took on long ago when our family began to grow well beyond the norm. Shannon had multiple friends at our local store. They delighted not only in her infectious smile but also in her glaringly obvious enthusiasm. Shannon loves nothing more than great colorful globes of air. Balloons are enough to set her to squealing. Our store had balloons of one sort or another at the end of virtually every aisle. And as I pushed the buggy from one section to the other, Shannon would reach out her hands, stretching and giggling at the mere presence of the balloons. She didn't come for cookies and cakes, candies and sugar-coated cereals. She came for the balloons. And as we began to check out, the good folks there would invariably give her one. Shannon would wrap one hand around the very base of the balloon, bury the other thumb deep in her mouth, and peacefully hold the balloon immediately in front of her face all the way home.

Strictly speaking, however, balloons are not necessary. Like baby Trixie from the "Hi and Lois" comic strip, Shannon has developed a love affair with sunbeams. As the slices of light descend on her crib, illuminating the dancing dust particles, it is her joyous habit to scratch the sheet and laugh. She will pat the warm spot where the sun hits, amused and delighted at God's own light show.

On a slightly more sophisticated note, music lights her up, but seemingly only live music. Play a CD or the car radio, and she is disinterested. Play the piano, however, and she will sit on the ground and listen. When the family sings together in family worship, she again lights up. We are all more mindful of God's astonishing kindness to us when Shannon's face beams as we sing together "Amazing Grace."

It was precisely because we think this simple joy is something we should grow out of that Jesus calls us to be like children. It is better to see balloons as droplets of joy than helium trapped inside Mylar. It is better to see a sunbeam as a blade of heavenly grass than electrons traveling at 186,000 miles a second. It is better to hear the voices of angels in a family singing off-key than to just hear a family singing off-key. Her perspective is the right one, the one I am to learn from her.

The blessings we enjoy in having Shannon in our lives, the lessons we learn by sitting at her feet, do not keep us from looking with hope to that day when she will be made well. When she was first diagnosed, from one perspective Denise and I didn't know if she would ever walk. From another perspective, we knew not only that she would walk but also that she would dance. We looked forward in hope to that day when, at the great wedding feast, the one Man who loves her more than we do will dance with her.

In His grace, however, we are not left merely hoping and waiting. Instead God has been gracious enough to let us have a taste of the future that awaits us. For we are not, as we mature sophisticates might think, a time-bound people. The work of Christ allows us to traverse through history and leap forward into the future consummation, the fullness of His Kingdom.

For more than a decade I wrote a column for *Tabletalk* magazine titled "Coram Deo," which is Latin for "before the face of God." My goal with each column was to remind my readers that we live all our days in the presence of God. That reality, however, doesn't undo the reality that when we gather together for corporate worship, we are, in a sense, drawing closer still to Him. That is especially true when we come to the Lord's Table. The Temple in Jerusalem reflected this reality. The outer court, the Court of the Gentiles, was designed specifically to communicate the presence of God with His people. Everyone everywhere was allowed in this area, which reflected the presence of both God and humanity in the broader world. The Holy Place, however, was that part of the Temple restricted to believers, those in covenant with God. This reflects our own places of worship, where God's people gather to renew covenant with Him. At the center of the Temple was the Holy of Holies. There, only once each year could one man, the high priest, enter. It was the veil that separated the Holy Place from the Holy of Holies that was torn in two, top to bottom, at the death of Christ on the cross.

When we draw near to God in and through the Lord's Supper, we are, in a manner of speaking, coming into the Holy of Holies. Consider what Paul says:

> You have not come to the mountain that may be touched and that burned with fire, and to blackness and darkness and tempest, and the sound of a trumpet and the voice of words, so that those who heard it begged that the word should not be spoken to them anymore. (For they could not endure what was commanded: "And if so much as a beast touches the mountain, it shall be stoned or shot with an

> arrow." And so terrifying was the sight that Moses said, "I am exceedingly afraid and trembling.")
>
> HEBREWS 12:18-21

This, we are told, is where we are *not* going. Sinai served as a symbol of the reality. But in biblical terms, the reality is always more real, more intense, than the symbol. We are taken someplace far more terrifying than Mount Sinai:

> You have come to Mount Zion and to the city of the living God, the heavenly Jerusalem, to an innumerable company of angels, to the general assembly and church of the firstborn who are registered in heaven, to God the Judge of all, to the spirits of just men made perfect, to Jesus the Mediator of the new covenant, and to the blood of sprinkling that speaks better things than that of Abel.
>
> HEBREWS 12:22-24

When we come to the Lord's Table, we do not do so in southwest Virginia or in Orlando, Florida. We do not go wherever we might be. Instead we are all lifted up, our hearts taken to the true and eternal Mount Zion. We traverse dimensions so that we might meet with the souls of those made perfect and with Jesus, the Mediator of the new covenant.

My own perspective, however, is that at the table we enter not only into a different place but also into a different time.

We need to think through not only *where* we are but *when* we are. Now to be sure, when we come to the table, it is right and fitting that we should remember what brought us here. We are right to remember that the body we are eating was broken by our own sins, the blood spilled for our own sins. We ought to remember that day when Jesus was crucified, remembering our place there, that we spit on Him, that we drove the nails into His hands.

We are not, however, recrucifying Him. That was done once for all. And we are not only to look back. Instead, we are also brought forward in time. That is, we enter into the fullness of the Kingdom. Remember that all of history is the outworking of the first war, the battle between the seed of the woman and the seed of the serpent. When Adam and Eve sinned, God declared war on the serpent and promised that a day would come when his head would be crushed by the bruised heel of the Son. History is the completion of that battle, the bringing to fullness of that promise.

At the table we put down our weapons. We come not in a context of war but of peace or rest. When we come, our Lord has prepared a table for us in the presence of our enemies (see Psalm 23:5). What is, after all, the fullness of the Kingdom? Is it not the glory of having His peace declared on us, which He does at the table? (This was the pattern of the Old Testament sacrificial system as well. It was true that the animal represented a substitute for the sins of the one making the offering. But then the forgiving Lord expressed His forgiveness and blessing in sharing a covenant meal with the repentant.) So, is not the fullness of the Kingdom drawing near to our Lord? And isn't the marriage feast of the Lamb feasting with Jesus? At the table we enter into heaven and into eternity.

It is for this very reason that we do not have to wait to see our precious little girl healed. In our church it has been our habit to celebrate the Lord's Supper every week. Row by row, families come forward and kneel, receiving the bread and the wine. When you have eight children with different ages, strengths, and abilities, there are thousands of different permutations on how this can get done. The oldest daughter might carry the baby, with Mom directing the preschoolers. The firstborn son might help Mom up the aisle. We had no set rules for how we got there, except one—Daddy takes Shannon.

I always bring my little girl to the table, even though she does not eat. I bring her with complete confidence that there she is well. Each time, as we kneel there, I whisper two gospel truths into my little girl's ear. I tell her, "Shannon, Jesus is here. Jesus is here, sweetheart, and Jesus loves you." Because I believe that in eternity, we have already entered into the consummation of the Kingdom, I believe in turn that she is healed. I believe therefore that she is able to understand perfectly what I am telling her. I am so persuaded of this truth that I have found myself praying an unusual prayer. When I come to the table, this is what I pray:

> *Lord, I give You thanks that You have brought us into the heavenlies and into eternity. My eyes see the* same

> *building I see every other day of the week. My internal clock registers that it is a Sunday morning. But these things can and do err. You have lifted us up, and I give You thanks. I give You thanks for Your declaration of peace upon us, that You love us unfailingly. I thank You also that You have here and now made my little girl well. I know, Lord, that when I speak these words to her, You are here, and that You love her; I know she is quite capable of turning to me and speaking with the utmost clarity and joy, "I know, Daddy. I have always known." Though I know You have made her able to do this, my prayer, Father, is that You would give me this honor, this blessing. Please, do not let her speak these words to me, so that I might be blessed to be able to believe them anyway. Keep her healed lips shut so that I might be able to walk by faith.*

A child knows how to pray. A child understands instinctively that a father knows better. When Jesus prayed at Gethsemane, "Nevertheless not My will, but Yours, be done" (Luke 22:42), He prayed as a wise child would. Jesus was saying nothing more than, "You know best, Daddy, and I trust You." I seek to exhibit, by His grace, that same spirit in that prayer. What I have found is that God knows exactly how to answer my prayer.

It is true enough that there has never been a Sunday when Shannon opened her lips and said those words to me. She does open her lips, but only to smile. That doesn't mean, however, that the Lord has left her mute. No, Shannon speaks to me every time we come to the Lord's Table. Or, rather, someone speaks through her. For when I look into my little girl's eyes there, my heart hears these words: *I am indeed here, R. C. And I do love Shannon. But I want you to know, I love you, too.*

Each week God speaks to both of us. And we, like Peter, James, and John on the Mount of Transfiguration, want nothing more than to stay in that moment of transcendence, to build booths, and to rejoice in the revelation of God's glory. We are tasting heaven, and we ache to remain. Our Lord, however, calls us to return to the battle, to return to the here and now so that we might labor faithfully to bring together heaven and earth, time and eternity. His promise as He calls us to descend from the true Mount Zion, is that we are welcome to come back, to feast with Him again.

When Jesus prayed at Gethsemane, "Nevertheless not my will, but Yours, be done," He prayed as a wise child would. Jesus was saying nothing more than, "You know best, Daddy, and I trust you."

Shannon is not just my little girl. She is also my big sister. She is the one who walks most closely with our common older Brother. She teaches me who He is and how tenderly He loves us both. She is the one who shows me how to better obey Him by trusting in His grace, by wondering at His power, and by rejoicing in His love. She is the one who teaches me how to be like a child, to be what our Father calls us to be. I sometimes wonder whether she is closer to heaven, better able to see through the veil, because she is younger than us or perhaps because in another sense she is more mature as she is closer to her homegoing than the rest of us. Perhaps it is both. Either way, Shannon is my spiritual better. I hope one day to be just like her, when I grow down.

9

THE CALL TO GOD'S PRESENCE

David danced before the Lord with all his might.

2 SAMUEL 6:14

JESUS' CALL TO BECOME LIKE CHILDREN isn't simply a call to cultivate childlike traits we've discussed in previous chapters. Certainly such traits as wonder, trust, and joy are part of the picture, but becoming childlike is so much more. Jesus is calling us to act here and now with the mind-set and emotions we will experience in full when we enter the glory of God's presence in eternity. To do that, we need to have a proper understanding of who God is. Too many of us approach Him with our own unexamined notions of His character.

We live in an age when the character of God has been eclipsed not only in the world but also in the church. God, if He is considered at all, is presented to us as safe, benign.

Often we have lost any sense of the transcendence of God as we have, in a purported interest to bring in the lost, smoothed over His "rough edges" and instead fashioned an idol with our own hands. We have declawed God, silencing His roar and creating a "tame" lion. The world and the church need to wake up, to remember the weightiness, the glory, of God. My father's passion over the years has been to awaken as many people as possible to the holiness of God in all its fullness.

It's always difficult to express what God's holiness is because there's really nothing on earth that can be compared with God and His glory. That's why my father dedicated his entire life to that goal. I find C. S. Lewis's depiction of Aslan in the Chronicles of Narnia helpful in imagining how different God is from what I experience here in Florida in the twenty-first century. In that series of fictional books, Lewis illustrates Aslan's "otherness" in ways that abstract theological terms cannot express. When the Pevensie children are first introduced to the idea of Aslan, Mr. Beaver is eager to point out that the lion is not at all safe. However, all we have to go by at that point in the story are the hushed words of this faithful forest animal. Later, in *The Silver Chair*, Jill Pole, led into Narnia by her classmate Eustace Scrubb, meets Aslan with precious little forewarning. Eustace has fallen off the edge of a cliff as a result of Jill's own foolishness. Before he plummets to his death, however, a lion bounds to the edge of the cliff and blows with such force that Jill's friend is carried away, out of sight. Then the lion turns and walks into the forest.

Jill is unsure of what to do, but soon enough she is distracted by a horrible thirst. From the forest she can hear a babbling brook that might provide a drink, but what has become of the lion? As Jill's desperation for a drink grows, she begins to make her way toward the brook, and so, she meets Aslan:

> She stood as still as if she had been turned into stone, with her mouth wide open. And she had a very good reason; just on this side of the stream lay the lion.
>
> It lay with its head raised and its two fore-paws out in front of it, like the lions in Trafalgar Square. She knew at once that it had seen her, for its eyes looked straight into hers for a moment and then turned away - as if it knew her quite well and didn't think much of her. . . .
>
> "Are you not thirsty?" said the Lion.
>
> "I'm dying of thirst," said Jill.
>
> "Then drink," said the Lion. . . .
>
> "Will you promise not to—do anything to me, if I do come?" said Jill.
>
> "I make no promise," said the Lion.

Just by watching, by looking, by listening, Jill knows that fear is the appropriate response to the Lion. He, on the other hand, apart from welcoming her to come and drink, does nothing to assuage her fears. He does not purr like a kitten or acquiesce to her request that he not do anything to harm her. Her desperation, however, eventually prompts her to ask, whether out of fear or hope we aren't told, a more direct question: "Do you eat girls?"

Here is the place and time for Aslan to put an end to the charade. Here he should laugh at Jill's fears and assure her that she has nothing at all to be afraid of. But the ridiculous question she has asked reveals a stunning lack of understanding of just who Aslan is.

Aslan does correct her, but not in the way we might expect: "'I have swallowed up girls and boys, women and men, kings and emperors, cities and realms,' said the Lion. It didn't say this as if it were boasting, nor as if it were sorry, nor as if it were angry. It just said it."

Here again, in something as "safe" as a children's story, Lewis expresses through the Aslan character what the otherness of God, the set-apart, transcendent authority of the Lord of heaven and earth might feel like to us. This is Yahweh, "I AM that I AM," taken on flesh in Narnia. He is not a tame lion; He is the God of the unexpected. His ways are not our ways, His thoughts not our thoughts.

God communicates that same otherness through His people, and through that, brings His children closer to Him. While we as Christians are all called to be holy, to be set apart, we are also called to not hide our lights under bushels, to live out our faith in the world. In the tiny town of Abingdon, Virginia, the members of Saint Peter Church, where I served for many years, did just that. The town was home to one local coffee shop that our members quickly adopted as an unofficial hangout. Friends met there. The elders of the church often met there. The senior pastor treated the shop as his office.

Serving up the coffee was a young single mom. Though she always provided service with a smile, her life had not been an easy one. Although not a believer, she soon found herself intrigued as she watched the members of our church. She made a point to engage us in conversation, and our pastor and others from the church did the same with her. Eventually our pastor invited this young woman to his family's home for dinner. There, the pastor, his wife, and their five children did what they always did. They enjoyed a typically amazing meal, and afterward the family turned their attention to a time of worship.

There was no forced, canned "close" on the worship time that night, no attempt to elicit from their guest a decision to follow Christ. There was, in fact, no close at all. More casual conversation at the coffee shop was followed by another casual invitation for dinner. At that point, the young lady confessed what she called the "oddness" of what she witnessed among our members and at the pastor's home. Still no close. It was at the third dinner that the young lady seemed determined to barge right into the Kingdom: she asked about Jesus, His death, her sins, and His grace.

And God brought her into the Kingdom. The church welcomed her warmly. She began an active prayer life, and within a few months we saw one of those prayers answered as a godly young single man in the church began to express an interest in her. A few months later the two were married. When we gathered for that wedding, we danced. That congregation is given to dancing—the Virginia reel, the Patty-Cake Polka, and other group dances—and it was my habit to remind the congregation of why we do this. Our dancing together, husbands and wives, toddlers and grandparents, is designed to express to the watching world our gratitude for God's grace. It is designed to welcome strangers. How much more did we dance to celebrate this stranger—this young lady—being brought into the Kingdom. We also dance to remind ourselves of God's grace. Most important of all, however, we dance to give God pleasure. We remember that our Father delights in nothing more than our joyful dance of gratitude before Him. Here we were experiencing the grand paradox: God, who is set apart in His holiness, draws near to us. He gives us life and causes us to become set apart, distinct, other. That difference, or "otherness," is often the very power that draws people in. We are all Cinderellas, brought to God's magnificent ball by powers beyond our comprehension—and the clock never strikes twelve!

It may well be the greatest glory of God's otherness, the greatest expression of His holiness, that the God we serve is not the God of either/or but rather the God of both/and. He can live in such paradox. The devil must always play a zero-sum game, because he can work only with what is. God, on the other hand, speaks reality into existence. His fullness never runs low. The three-ness of the persons of the godhead—Father, Son, and Holy Spirit—are together the one of the essence of the godhead. He can take the God-ness of the Son and bring it into union with the Man-ness of the New Adam.

In the same way, this God who sits in the heavenlies, exalted and lifted up, whose ways are not ours, expressed His "set apart" nature in part by, surprisingly, drawing near to us. What makes Yahweh Yahweh and not a tame, aloof, distant god is that He is the God of Abraham, Isaac, and Jacob. Perhaps the most shockingly transcendent thing about the God we worship is that He is pleased to stoop down to us, to draw near, to know us, love us, walk with us, and call us all by name.

The same untamed Aslan who refuses to set Jill Pole's fears aside is captured in a beautiful moment of immanence in the first of the stories, *The Lion, the Witch and the Wardrobe*. In this story, Aslan, Son of the Emperor-beyond-the-Sea, lays down his life for another person. Edmund Pevensie had left his brother and sisters, seeking to turn them over to the White Witch in exchange for candy, Turkish Delight. This act of betrayal, this fall into sin, forfeits Edmund's soul to the witch, but Aslan offers to take the place of Edmund and to suffer for him. With fiendish delight, the witch binds Aslan, drives her dagger into his heart, and leaves him, still bound, where he died.

Perhaps the most shockingly transcendent thing about the God we worship is that He is pleased to stoop down to us, to draw near, to know us, love us, walk with us, and call us all by name.

Like our own story, however, Lewis's story does not end

there. As Lucy and Susan Pevensie mourn Aslan's death, field mice descend upon Aslan's body and begin gnawing at the ropes that bind him.

> And at last, one by one, the ropes were all gnawed through. . . .
>
> The girls cleared away the remains of the gnawed ropes. Aslan looked more like himself without them. Every moment his dead face looked nobler, as the light grew and they could see it better. . . .
>
> It was quite definitely early morning now, not late night.
>
> "I'm so cold," said Lucy.
>
> "So am I," said Susan. "Let's walk about a bit." . . .
>
> They walked to and fro more times than they could count between the dead Aslan and the eastern ridge, trying to keep warm. . . . At last, as they stood for a moment looking out towards the sea and Cair Paravel (which they could now just make out) the red turned to gold along the line where the sea and the sky met and very slowly up came the edge of the sun. At that moment they heard from behind them a loud noise—a great cracking, deafening noise as if a giant had broken a giant's plate.
>
> "What's that?" said Lucy, clutching Susan's arm.
>
> "I–I feel afraid to turn round," said Susan; "something awful is happening."

> "They're doing something worse to *Him*," said Lucy. "Come on!" And she turned, pulling Susan round with her.
>
> The rising of the sun had made everything look so different—all the colours and shadows were changed—that for a moment they didn't see the important thing. Then they did. The Stone Table was broken into two pieces by a great crack that ran down it from end to end; and there was no Aslan. . . .
>
> "Who's done it?" cried Susan. "What does it mean? Is it more magic?"

The deeper magic has made mourning turn to dancing as the girls realize that Aslan is once again alive. But what we shouldn't miss is that same spirit of joy in the one who becomes their dance partner:

> "Oh, children," said the Lion, "I feel my strength coming back to me. . . ." He stood for a second, his eyes very bright, his limbs quivering, lashing himself with his tail. Then he made a leap high over their heads and landed on the other side of the Table.
>
> Laughing, though she didn't know why, Lucy scrambled over it to reach him. Aslan leaped again. A mad chase began. Round and round the hill-top he led them, now hopelessly out of their reach, now letting them almost catch his tail, now diving

> between them, now tossing them in the air with his huge and beautifully velveted paws and catching them again, and now stopping unexpectedly so that all three of them rolled over together in a happy laughing heap of fur and arms and legs. It was such a romp as no one has ever had except in Narnia.

The great Aslan, the lion who is anything but tame, frolics with the Daughters of Eve, caught up in the wonder of his own resurrection. His joy is not austere but overflowing, not staid but giddy. Aslan—a picture of the Son of God—is playing cat and mouse with two little girls he loves.

This carefree outburst of delight is a reflection of another such outburst, though this one is captured in the pages of Scripture and offers a biblical example of how we should delight in the presence of God.

The Ark of the Covenant, the physical symbol of God's presence with His people, had earlier been captured in battle by the Philistines, who placed the Ark in their temple to their god Dagon. After the idols of Dagon are found prostrate before the Ark, the Philistines realize it is not going well for them and determine to send the Ark back to God's people, who receive it with great joy:

> David went and brought up the ark of God from the house of Obed-Edom to the City of David with gladness. And so it was, when those bearing the ark of the Lord had gone six paces, that he sacrificed

> oxen and fatted sheep. Then David danced before the LORD with all his might; and David was wearing a linen ephod. So David and all the house of Israel brought up the ark of the LORD with shouting and with the sound of the trumpet.
>
> 2 SAMUEL 6:12-15

The king's joy is not shared, however, by all those in his household. David's guileless dance of gratitude catches the attention of his wife, and she is not pleased: "Now as the ark of the LORD came into the City of David, Michal, Saul's daughter, looked through a window and saw King David leaping and whirling before the LORD; and she despised him in her heart" (v. 16).

This was no mere attack of embarrassment on Michal's part. We are told that she despised her own husband. Why? Because he forgot his royal dignity. He forgot his "place" in the broader culture. He forgot, in his celebration, the pomp and ceremony of his office and was seen doing so by the one person who would never forget such a thing: his wife, the daughter of the former king Saul.

The father of the Son of David, David himself, rejoices like a child, dancing not, as we are sometimes encouraged to do, as if no one were watching but as if his heavenly Father is watching. And indeed He is. David soon discovers, however, that while his heavenly Father was watching him dance and rejoice, his earthly wife was not pleased: "David returned to bless his household. And Michal the daughter of Saul came out to meet David, and said, 'How glorious was the king of Israel today, uncovering himself today in the eyes of the maids of his servants, as one of the base fellows shamelessly uncovers himself!'" (v. 20).

Michal's lack of respect for David, and thus her failure to remember his office, soon prompts David to remember his standing (vv. 21-22):

> David said to Michal, "It was before the Lord, who chose me instead of your father and all his house, to appoint me ruler over the people of the Lord, over Israel. Therefore I will play music before the Lord. And I will be even more undignified than this, and will be humble in my own sight. But as for the maidservants of whom you have spoken, by them I will be held in honor."

David wisely affirms the propriety, the wisdom, of being undignified before the Lord. And lest we are tempted to wonder just where God's sympathies lie in the midst of this domestic spat, we are told in the next verse, "Therefore Michal the daughter of Saul had no children to the day of her death" (v. 23).

The point of this text is not some romantic notion that we ought to always come before the presence of the Lord casually. The point is not to argue that God is most glorified in us when we approach Him in our most debased fashion. The text does remind us, however, that the glory of God, the transcendence of God, is not an argument against—or even a counterbalance to—His joy in drawing near to us. The God we serve judged the flippancy of Uzzah, who, when the Ark was being brought to Jerusalem on an oxcart, reached out (against God's express command) to steady the Ark when the oxen stumbled. God struck down Uzzah, killing him instantly (vv. 6-7). I suspect Uzzah's wife, children, and parents were well familiar not only with what happened to Nadab and Abihu, the sons of Aaron who offered up strange fire and were killed instantly, but also with the answer Moses gave to the distraught Aaron:

> Moses said to Aaron, "This is what the LORD spoke, saying:
> 'By those who come near Me I must be regarded
> as holy;
> And before all the people I must be glorified.'"
> So Aaron held his peace.
> LEVITICUS 10:3

The fact that God judges the flippancy of Uzzah, who made the egregious mistake of thinking the Ark would be desecrated by mere mud but could be protected by the polluted hands of a sinful man, does not undo the truth that He in turn judges the severe austerity of Michal.

To put my point in the plainest English: that we are called to fear God does not undo the equally vital truth that we are to delight in Him.

Even this, however, misses the truth. To speak the language of duty, while right and proper from one perspective, is to miss another important truth. We are not to rejoice in God merely because we owe it to Him. David did not look down at the arrival of the Ark and think to himself, *God will be mad at me if I don't throw caution to the wind and make a spectacle of myself. Because I owe this to Him, I am willing to do so, even though it will make Michal as mad as a hornet.* The call to delight in our heavenly Father is not one that can be rightly obeyed with bootstrap effort. One cannot grimly determine to rejoice in the grace of God. The only way to rejoice the way David did is to be overcome with emotion. David's joyous dance was true to who he was and true to how he felt about God. It was David becoming like a child, so much so that he insisted on giving in to his willingness, even his eagerness, to become undignified.

That God would strike Uzzah dead for effrontery and then turn and judge Michal for condemning the familiarity of David is not evidence of a contradiction. Rather it is more evidence of the constant paradox that the God we serve is alone the self-sufficient Creator and Lord over all things who condescends to us as His children, loving us and rejoicing in us as an earthly father does with his children. He is the Lion of Judah, who consumes whole realms and yet frolics in the grass with His children. That is a picture of the good news in the Scripture, made possible by God's grace shown in the life of Christ.

The fact that we have lived our lives under God's gracious,

tender care has not, sadly, multiplied our gratitude but muted it. If you're anything like me, you forget the all-important expression of thanks. How many times do we look back over decades of God's faithfulness to us, centuries of His faithfulness to our families, and gasp in awe? Too often God's good gifts distract us from contemplating His faithful love toward us. Instead of seeing all of this as God's extraordinary grace, we come to expect the comfort and joys that God gives us as the baseline, the measure of what we believe to be our due. When our comfort level drops below our expectations, we are shocked and angered, and even foolishly express our outrage to God Himself. When we throw such childish hissy fits, we too often comfort ourselves by reasoning that God is a big boy and He can take it. Yes, He can take it. But He is not the big boy we so often imagine. He is instead an infinite God, and He may very well not take it. We need to learn to guard our tongues—and use them to give thanks in all circumstances.

Not long ago I found myself making a difficult pastoral call. A dearly loved woman under my care had just been sent back to the hospital after her leukemia relapsed. Her condition was grave, and there was a very real possibility that she would not leave the hospital alive. Making matters worse, this woman is a wife and a mother to eight children. As we visited, she began to cry and expressed the weight of fear she was carrying. I asked what, among all the normal fears we might expect, was she afraid of.

She acknowledged her faith and her confidence about

eternity. She likewise affirmed that the process of dying wasn't the root of her fear. Her fear was for those left behind. She was concerned about the heartache her husband would feel. She was imagining the shadow that might intrude into her daughters' weddings, not having Mom there. She wept for her littlest boys, who would, should she be taken, grow up without her.

I acknowledged her fears. I agreed with her, first, that she would be in a place of great joy, where Jesus Himself would wipe away her tears. But I also agreed about the hardships that those left behind would face. They would mourn and weep for a season, and carry the scars of their loss all their days. I pointed out, however, that those pains would be softened by the knowledge of her joy, that her husband and children would find comfort in knowing that she was beyond pain, beyond fear, and in the very presence of God.

Because I am so close to this woman and know her children so well, I couldn't help but weep with her for the loss they might face. Then I explained that my own perspective was just a touch different, that the genuine grief they would have for their loss would be countered by the joy they would feel for what they had had. One cannot—or at least ought not—acknowledge the pain of loss without giving thanks for what has been given. My love for these children drives me to empathy for this potential loss. It in turn makes me stunned that their heavenly Father should have blessed them to have had this woman for a mother.

The children, I pray, will not be alone in this perspective.

The husband, whether that day comes sooner or later, will mourn his loss. He will also give thanks for what he has been given. He, too, is stunned that he should have been blessed to have this woman for a wife. I know this to be true because I am the husband of this saintly woman, who cries in fear for me and our children. I know because I am the father to those eight children, each of whom received immeasurable grace from God in having this woman for a mother.

My desire, however, is not just that I would remember to give thanks for *previous* blessings when God in His providence removes them. Instead I am called to give thanks not just in the midst of the hard providence but *for* the hard providence. When facing challenges, we don't rightly look back to days with fewer challenges and give thanks for them, then look forward with hope to days with fewer challenges and give thanks for those. Instead we give thanks for every day, for challenges and for the relief from those challenges, for blessings and the blessed removal of those blessings.

It isn't, in other words, merely a *comfort* when we walk through the valley of the shadow of death to know that God is with us, that He is holding our hands. Rather, it is a source of joy that He is holding our hands. The defining quality of the story isn't the valley; it is His presence in the valley. The valley is just a backdrop, a stage setting, because the real story is that we are walking with God. When Jesus' scarred hands wrap themselves around us and He holds us tight, when we look up to see His own tender tears splash down on us, how can we hear anything in the sound of His heartbeat but His unshakable love for us? Each beat sounds the truth: "I love you My child. I will love you forever. I will never leave you. I will never forsake you." How can we do anything but rejoice and give thanks?

Though I sit in a hospital room while deadly chemicals drip into the veins of the bride of my youth, she and I are both already living in a better country. We have already been welcomed into the Kingdom. We are already seated in the heavenly places in Christ Jesus. And He has already overcome the world. All that we lack, all that we need, are the eyes of children, so that we might see this glorious Kingdom. All we lack is the faith of a child that we might believe and see.

It isn't merely a comfort when we walk through the valley of the shadow of death to know that God is with us, that He is holding our hands. Rather, it is a source of joy that He is holding our hands.

Too often, as an adult, I'm tempted to drive a wedge between here and there, between then and now, between heaven and earth. Immersed in work and school schedules, in articles to write and lectures to give, I'm tempted to think the realities of heaven don't touch this earth.

Yet I know my future hope—indeed, the hope of my wife and of Darby, Campbell, Shannon, Delaney, Erin Claire, Maili, Reilly, and Donovan—is in a God who makes the future now. Though I sit in this hospital room in Orlando, I'm actually sitting in the presence of God Himself.

May I have the eyes of a child to see.

About the Author

R. C. Sproul Jr. served for eleven years as editor-in-chief of *abletalk* magazine. In 1996 he began Highlands Ministries and planted Saint Peter Presbyterian Church in southwestern Virginia. He is editor of *Every Thought Captive* magazine, a teaching fellow at Ligonier Ministries, and a visiting faculty member of Ligonier Academy of Biblical and Theological Studies. He and his wife, Denise, live in Orlando, Florida, with their eight children.

ABOUT LIGONIER MINISTRIES

Ligonier Ministries, founded in 1971 by Dr. R. C. Sproul, is an international Christian education organization that strives to help people grow in their knowledge of God and His holiness.

"We believe that when the Bible is taught clearly, God is seen in all His majesty and holiness—hearts are conquered, minds are renewed, and communities are transformed," Dr. Sproul says.

From its base near Orlando, Florida, Ligonier carries out its mission in various ways:

- By daily teaching on the *Renewing Your Mind with R. C. Sproul* radio broadcast, heard throughout the U.S. and internationally.
- By training and equipping young adults, laypeople, and pastors through the Ligonier Academy of Biblical and Theological Studies and Reformation Bible College.
- By producing solid, in-depth teaching resources, making them available online through the Ligonier.org website.
- By publishing *The Reformation Study Bible*.
- By publishing *Tabletalk*, a monthly theological/devotional magazine.
- By publishing and promoting books true to the historic Christian faith.
- By producing and promoting conferences.

www.ligonier.org | (800) 435-4343

CP0542

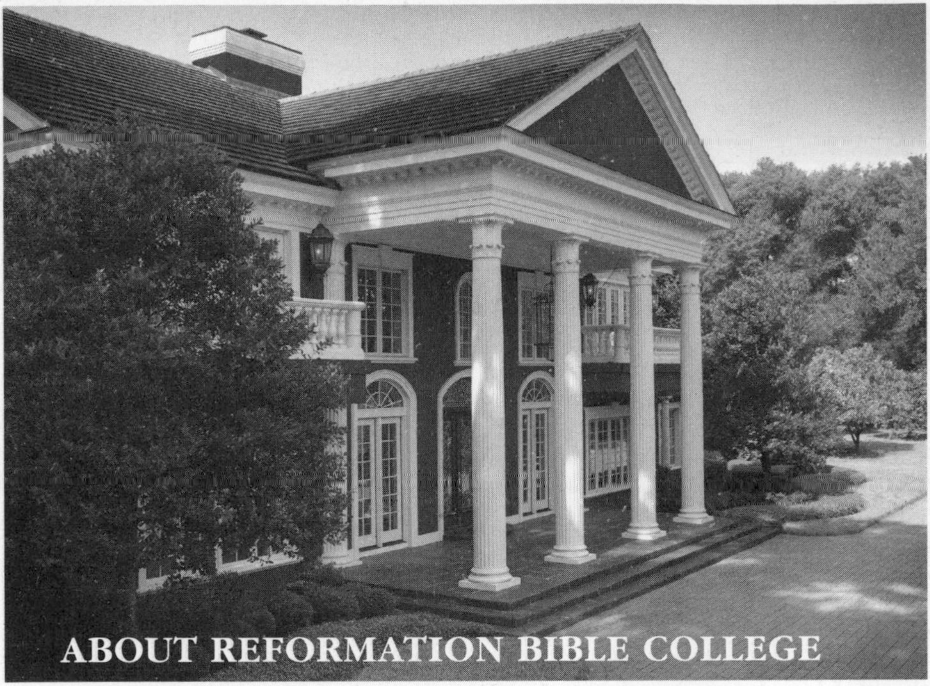

ABOUT REFORMATION BIBLE COLLEGE

Dr. R. C. Sproul Jr. is associate professor of philosophy and apologetics for Reformation Bible College (RBC) located near Orlando, Florida.

RBC unapologetically adheres to the historic Christian faith. We believe that literacy in theology and history is vital for a mature knowledge of Scripture and a discerning engagement with the world.

RBC's curriculum is intentionally designed to focus on the content of Scripture, the system of doctrine taught in Scripture, church history, and the great works of philosophy, literature, and music. RBC offers a two-year associate of arts degree and 3 four-year bachelor of arts degrees.

- Associate of Arts in Biblical and Theological Studies
- Bachelor of Arts in Biblical Studies
- Bachelor of Arts in Theological Studies
- Bachelor of Arts in Sacred Music

RBC is the encapsulation of everything Ligonier Ministries and its founder, Dr. R. C. Sproul, have valued and advanced for the past forty years. With God's help, we at Reformation Bible College want to pass on the knowledge of God and the things of God to the generations that follow.

Reformation Bible College

www.ReformationBibleCollege.org | 1-888-RBC-1517

CP0543

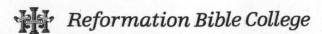